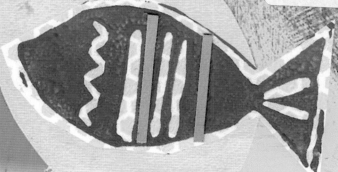

Doodle, IMAGINE, Draw

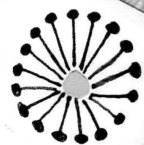

PaRragon

Bath • New York • Cologne • Melbourne • Delhi
Hong Kong • Shenzhen • Singapore • Amsterdam

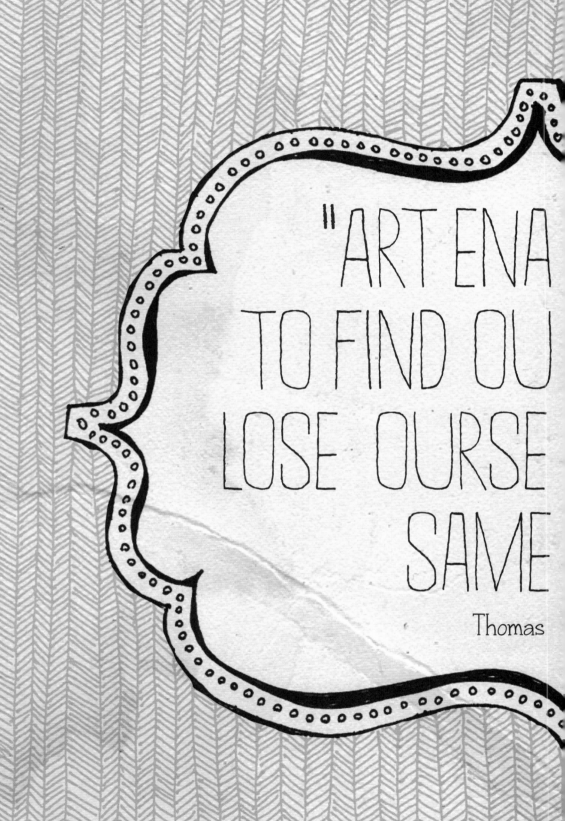

"ART ENA
TO FIND OU
LOSE OURSE
SAME

Thomas

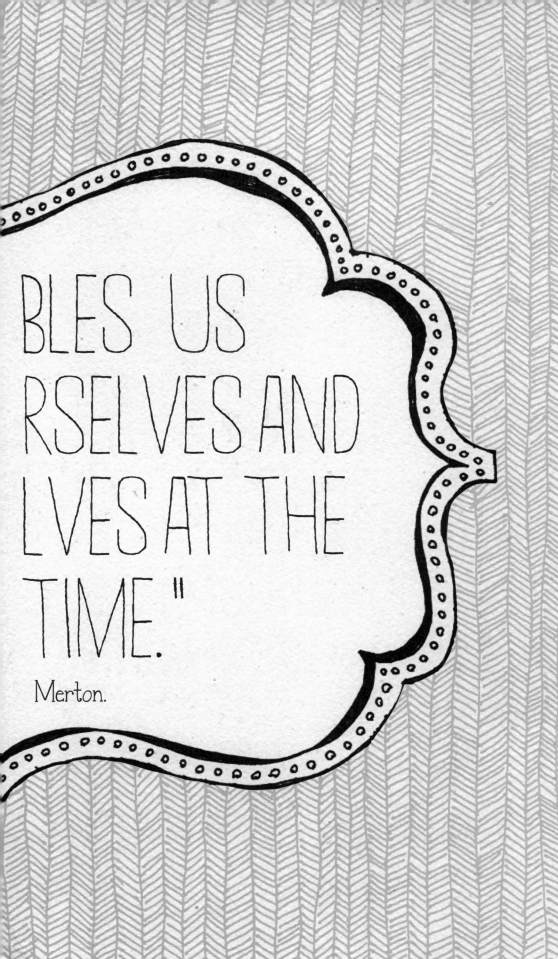

"BLES US
RSELVES AND
LVES AT THE
TIME."

Merton.

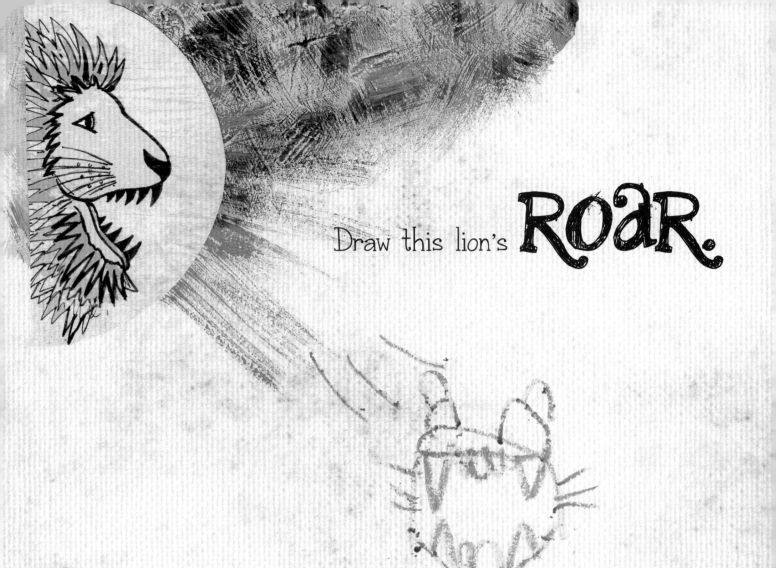

Draw this lion's **ROAR.**

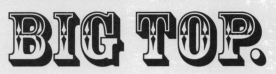

Draw the inside of this
BIG TOP.

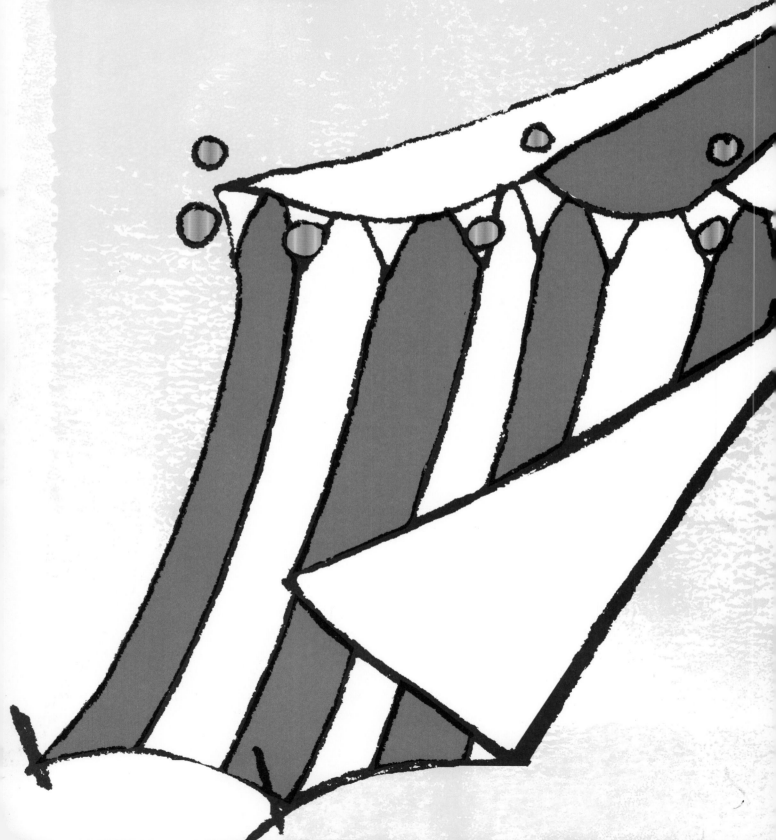

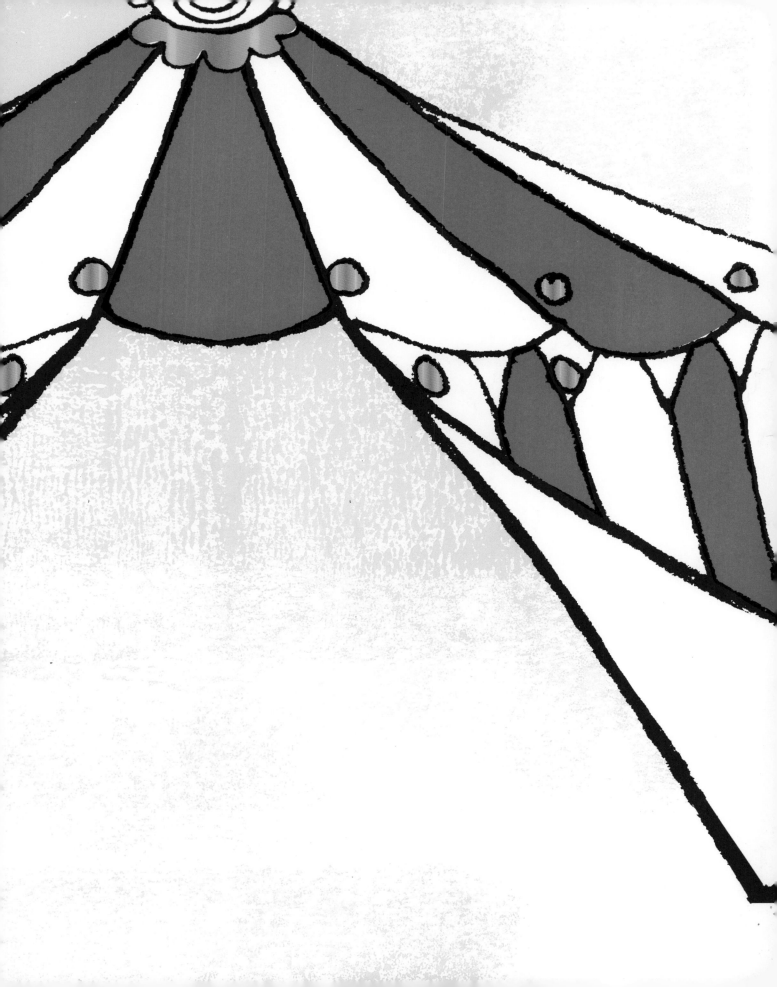

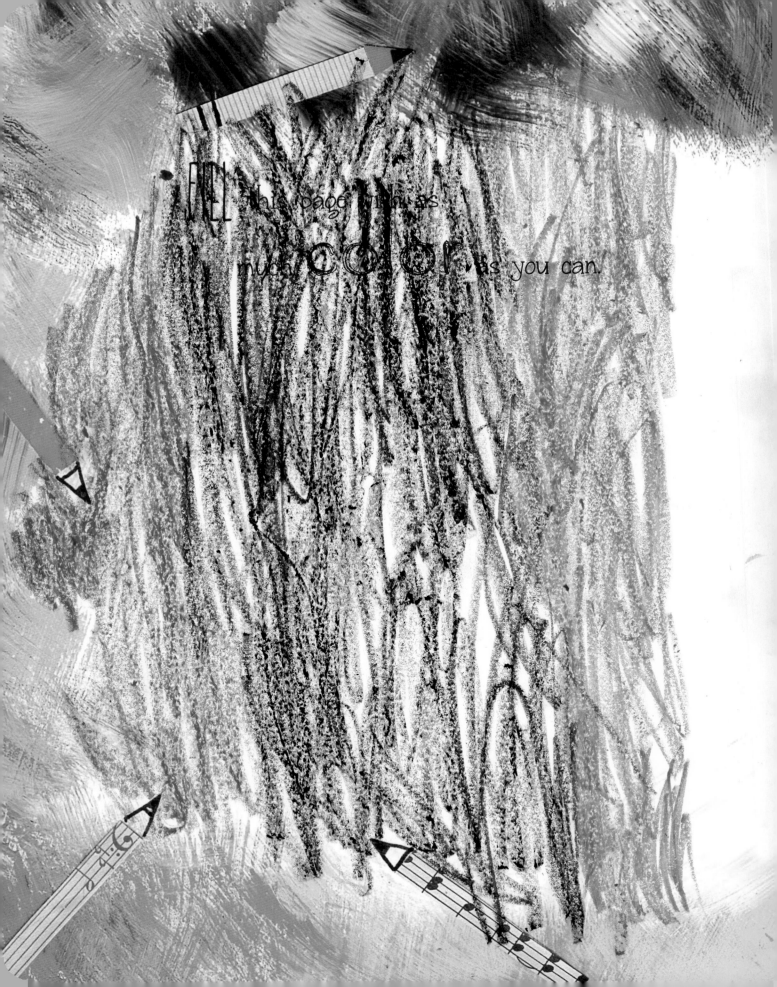

Fill this page with as much **color** as you can.

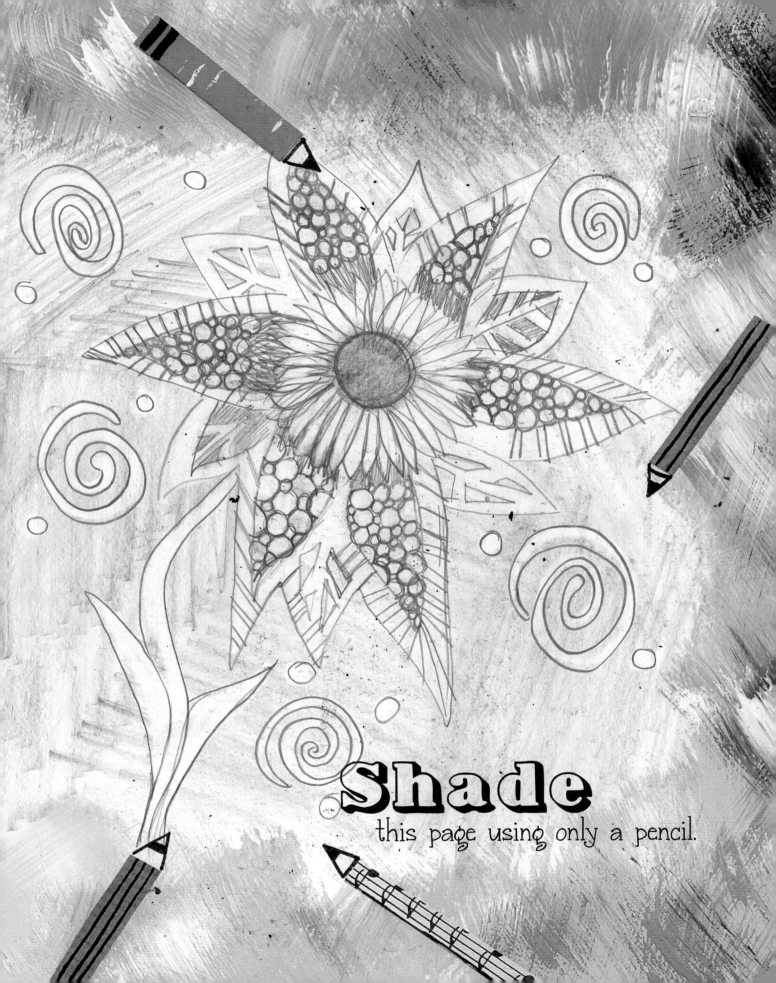

Shade

this page using only a pencil.

Draw something
massive!

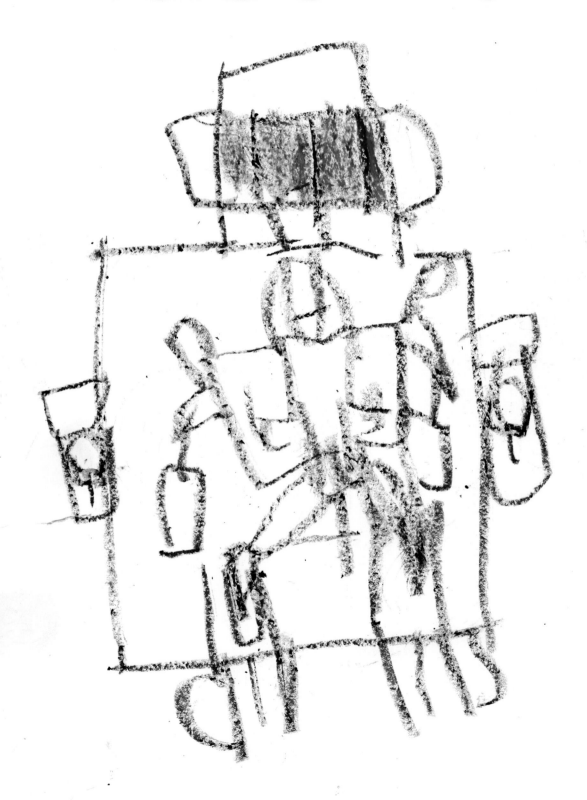

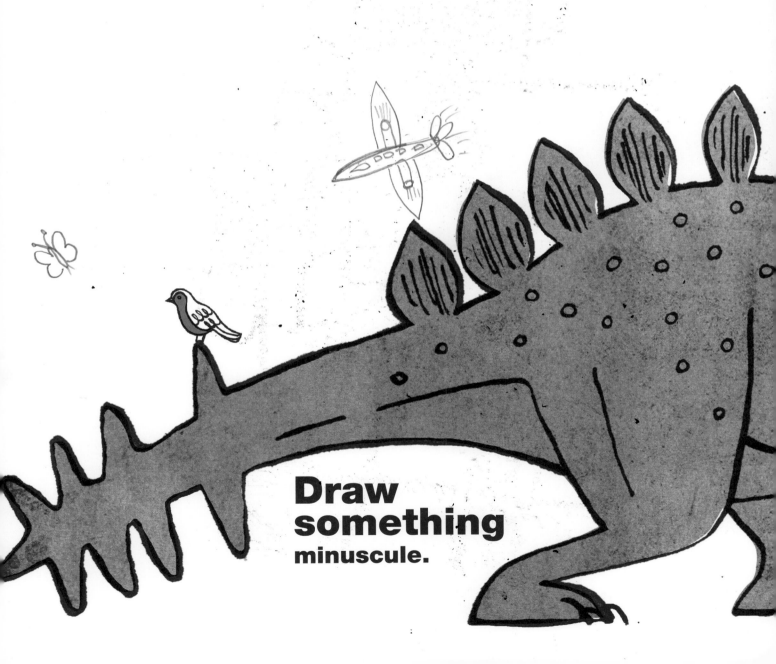

**Draw
something**
minuscule.

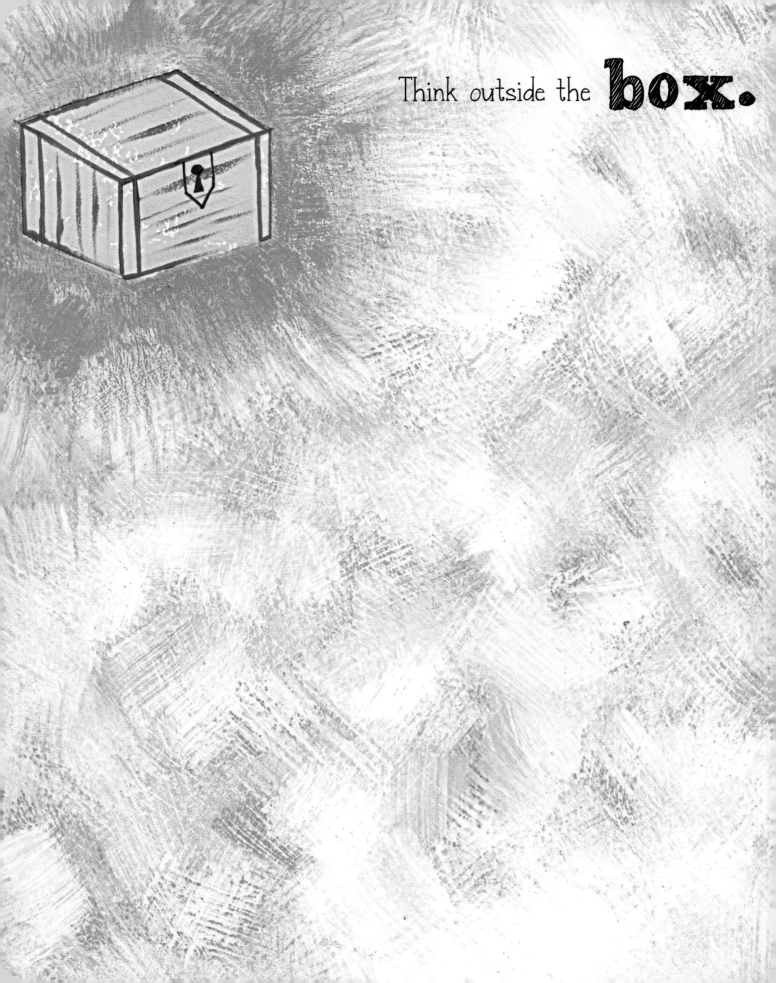

Think outside the **box.**

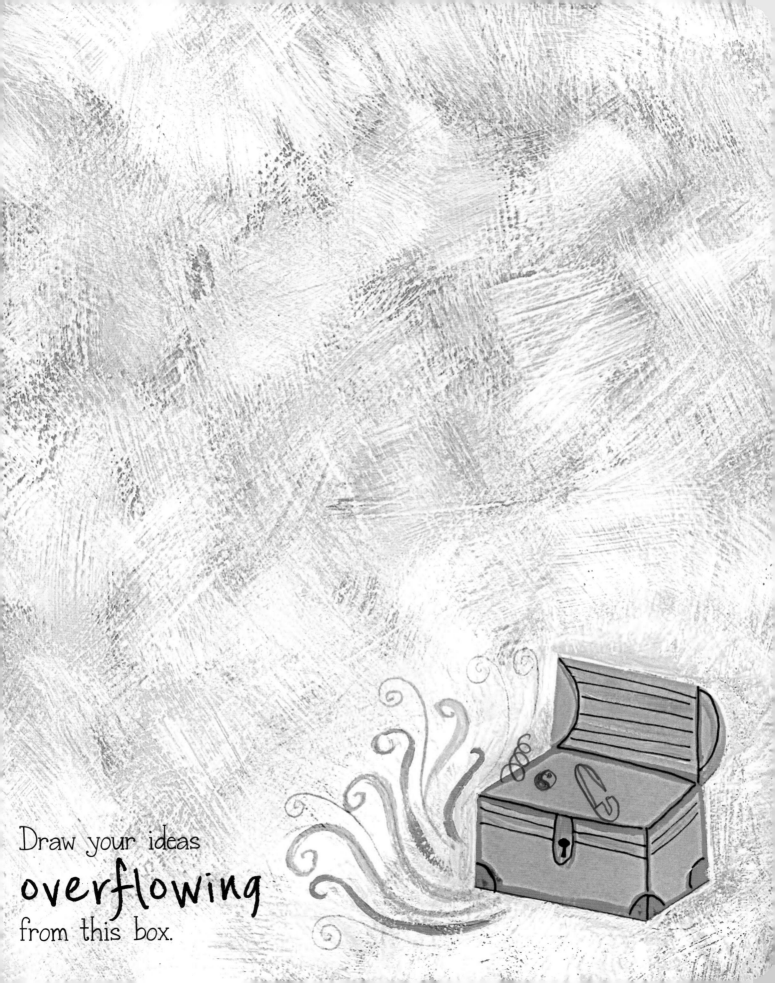

Draw your ideas **overflowing** from this box.

Make these pages into a MAZE.

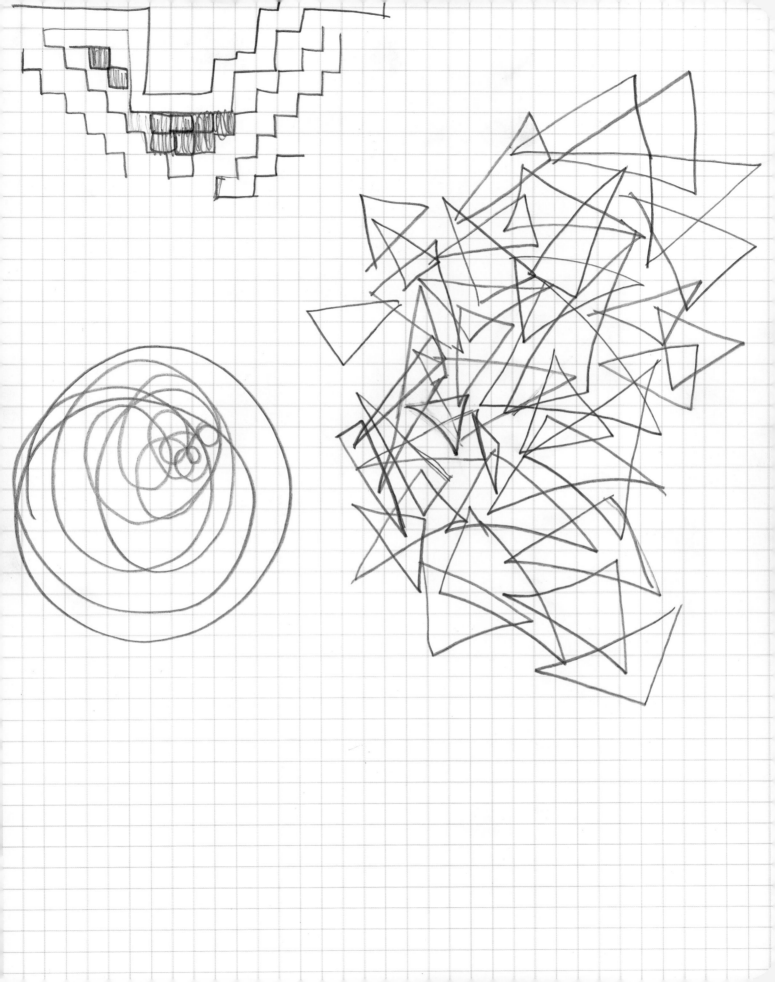

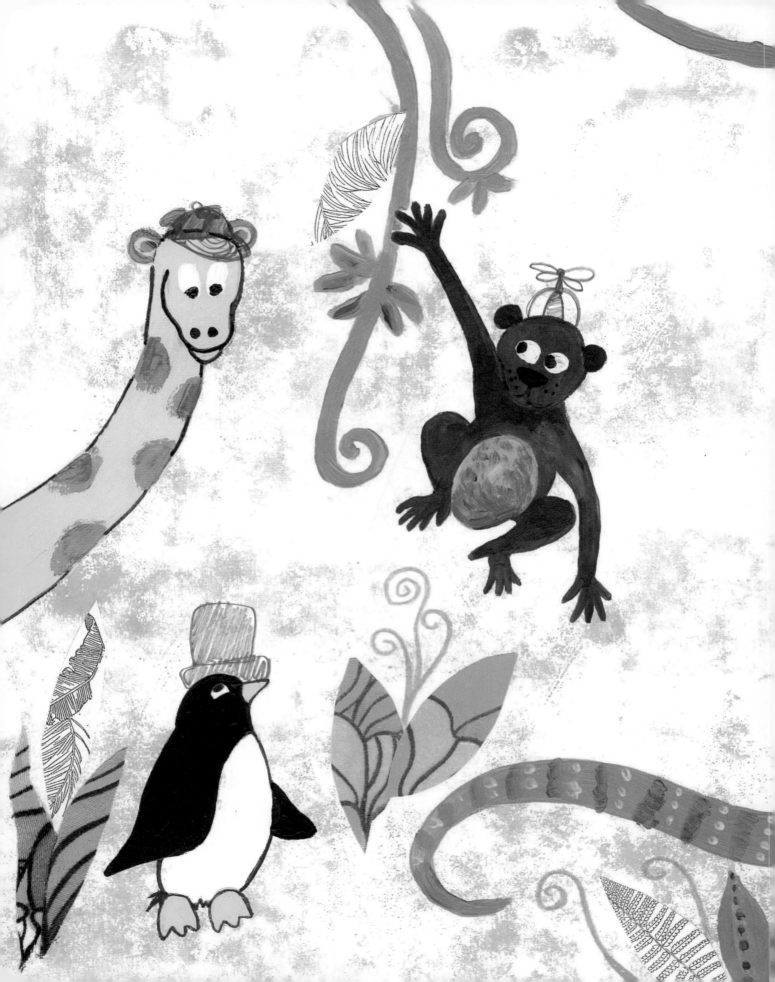

Add some HATS
to these animals.

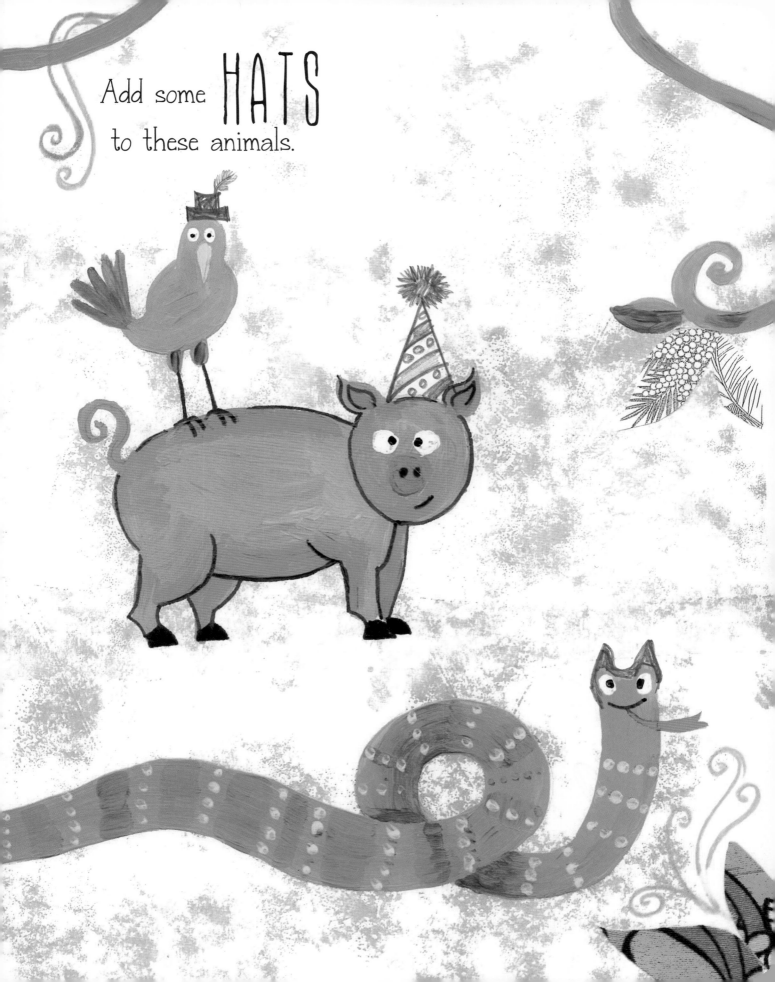

Fill these vases with flowers.

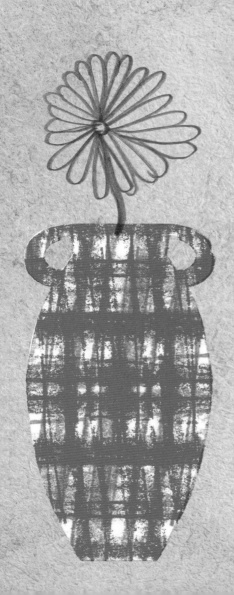

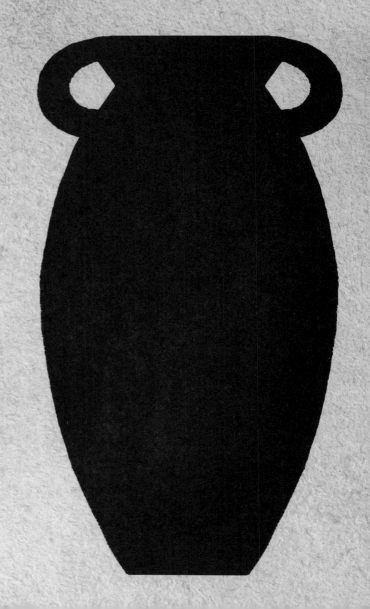

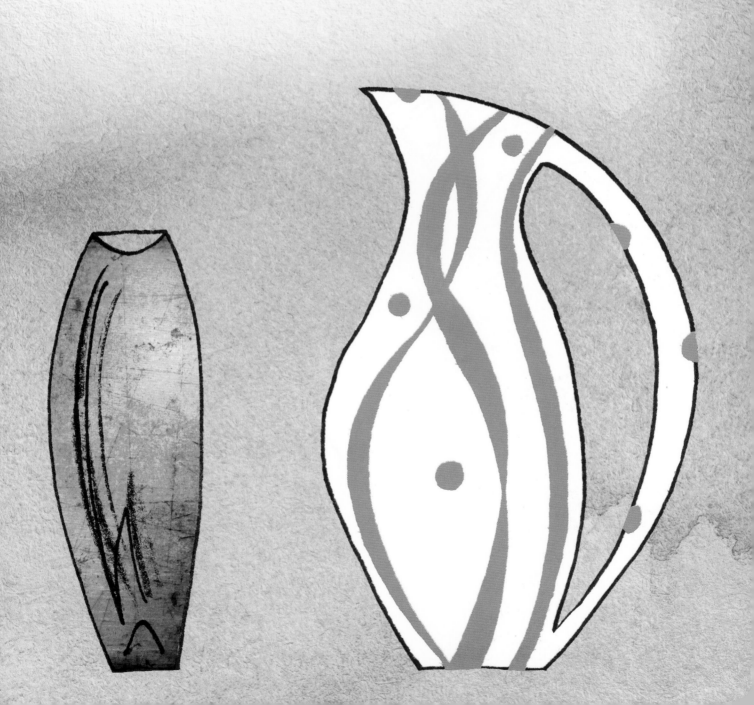

Design your own *everlasting knot.*

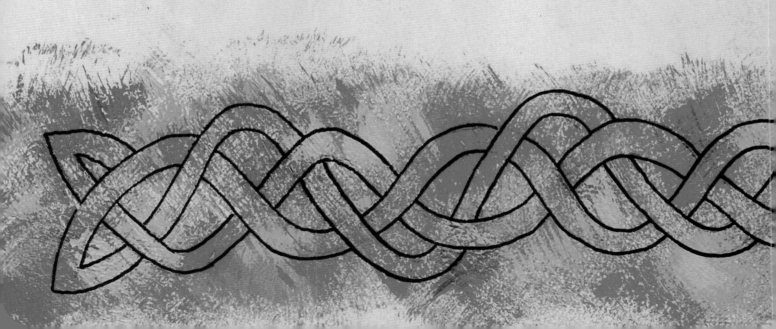

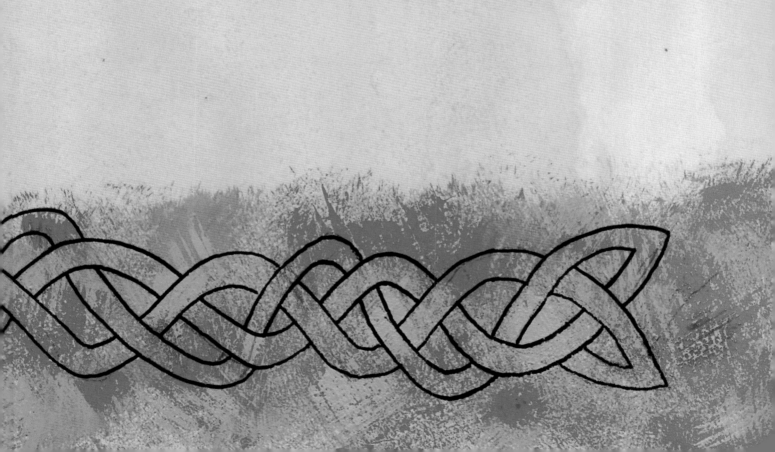

Fill these craft jars
with safety pins, thread, buttons, and other odds and ends.

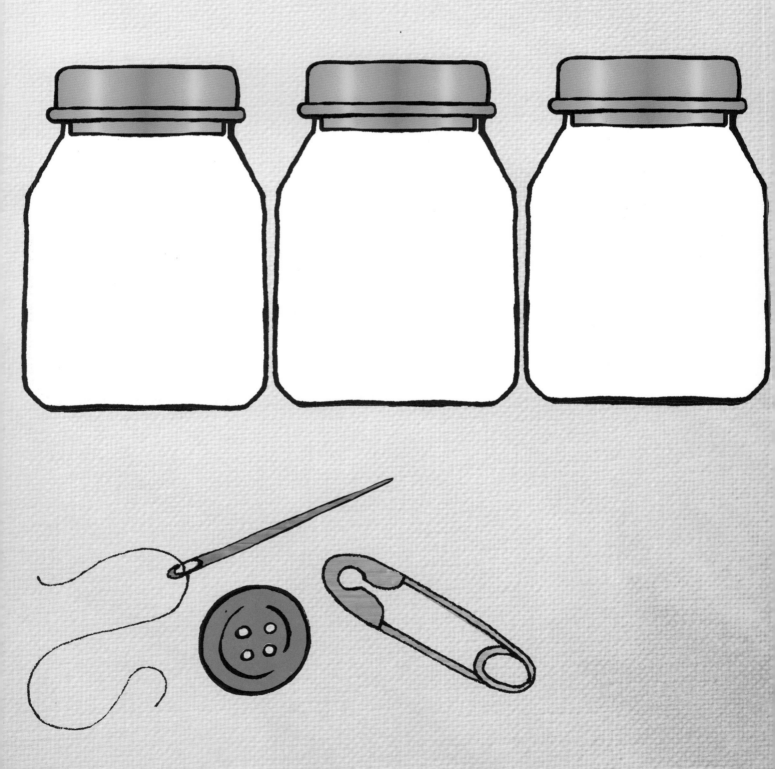

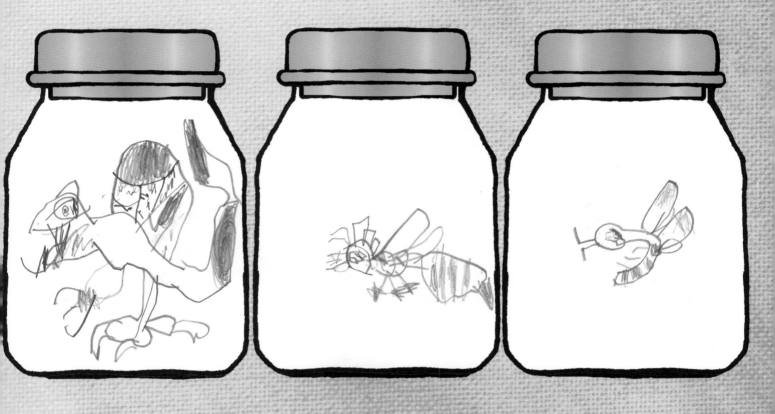

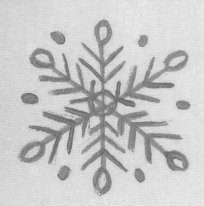

Draw your
favorite season.

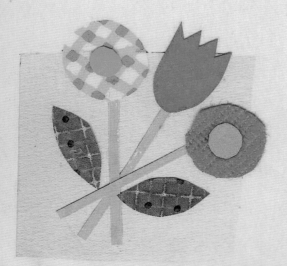

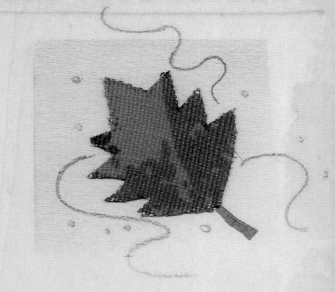

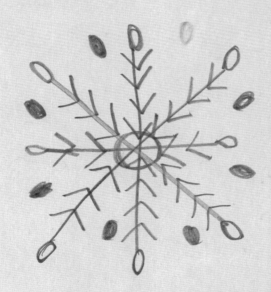

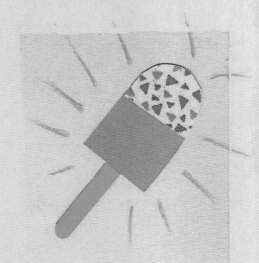

Draw your LEAST FAVORITE SEASON.

Draw an ASTRONAUT
floating in outer space.

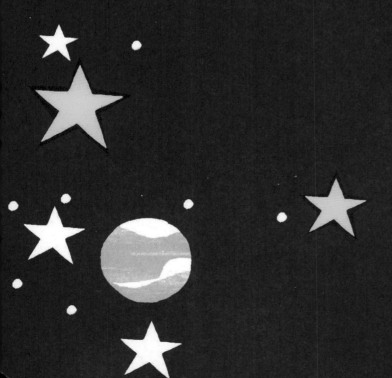

Add bodies to these eyes.

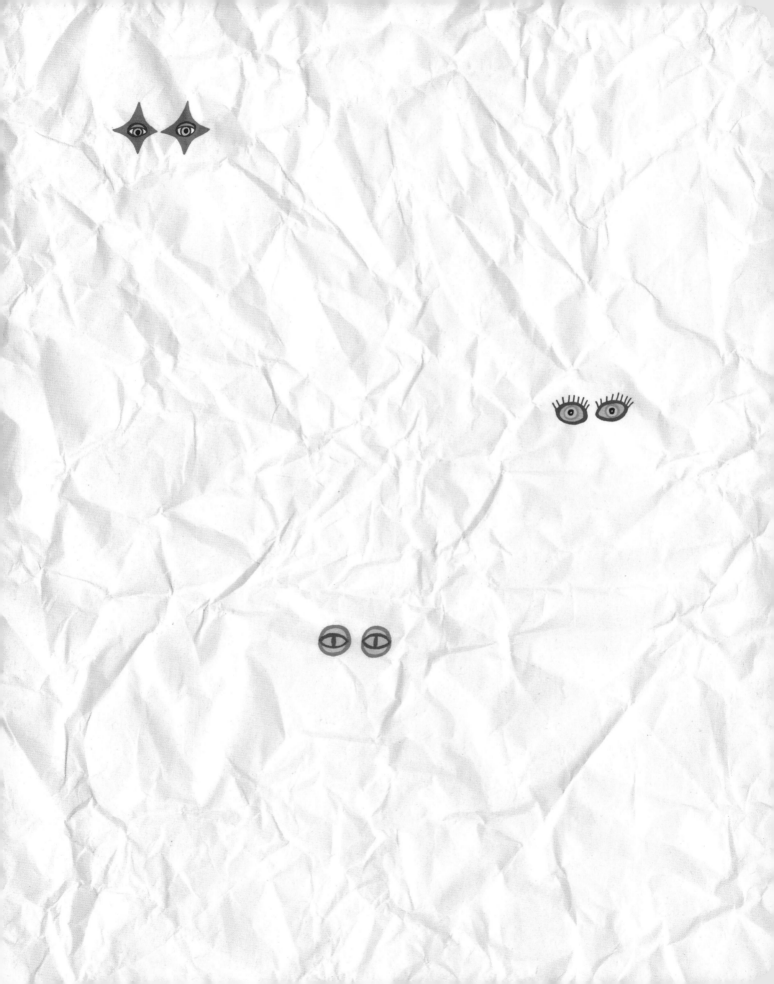

Draw the rest of this
elephant.

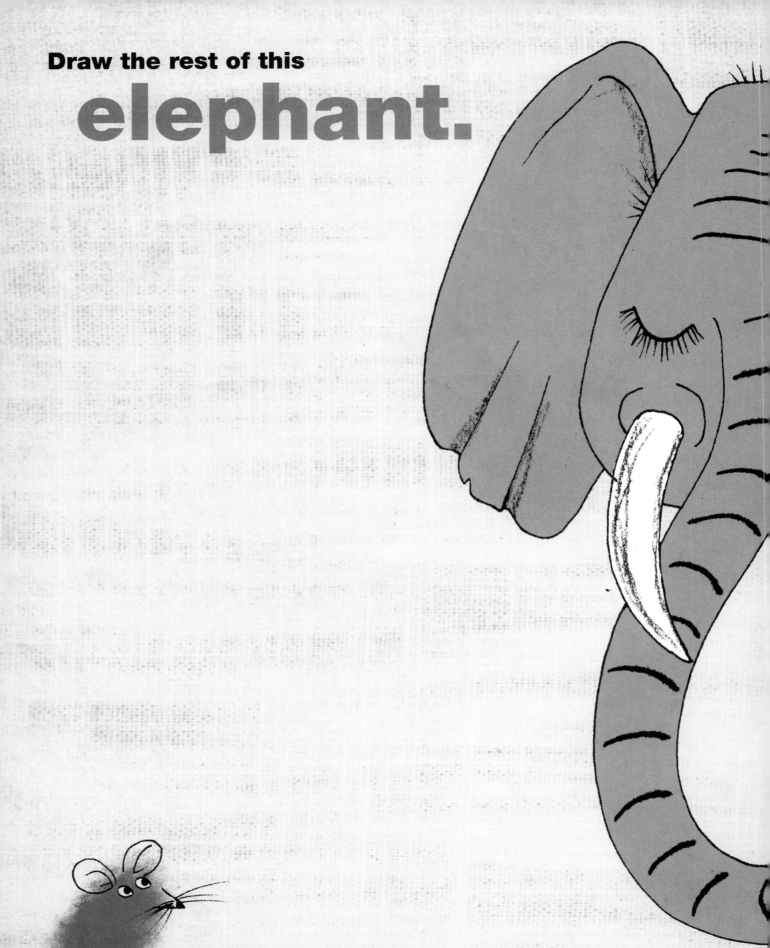

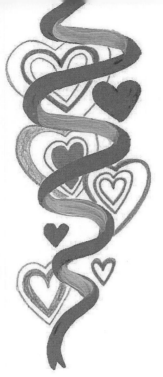

What does the *color red* look like when it's jealous?

What does the
color yellow look
like when it's **excited**?

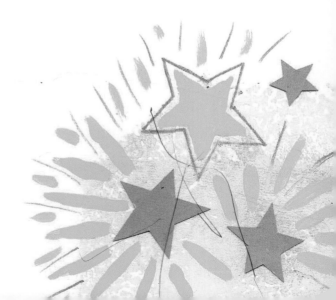

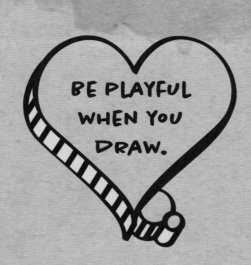

BE PLAYFUL
WHEN YOU
DRAW.

Draw a **ZIGZAG**
chasing a curve.

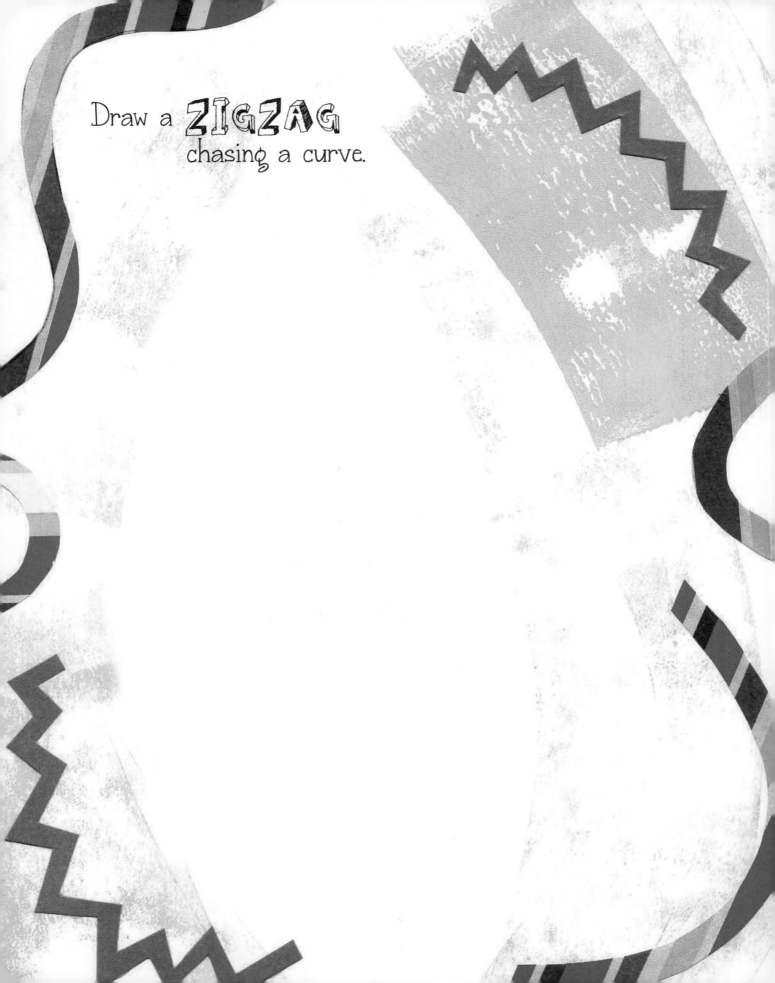

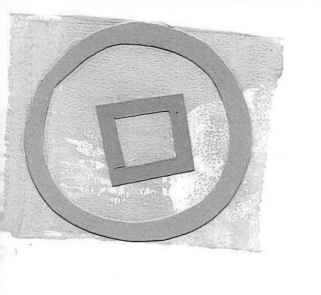

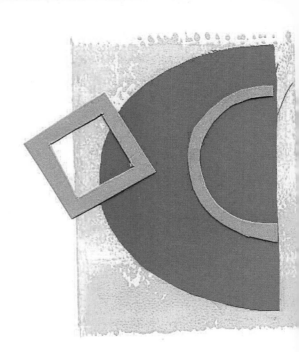

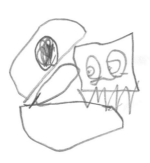

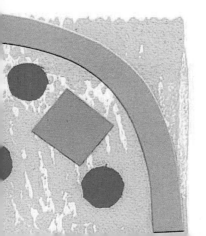

Draw a CIRCLE eating a square.

Design this couch.

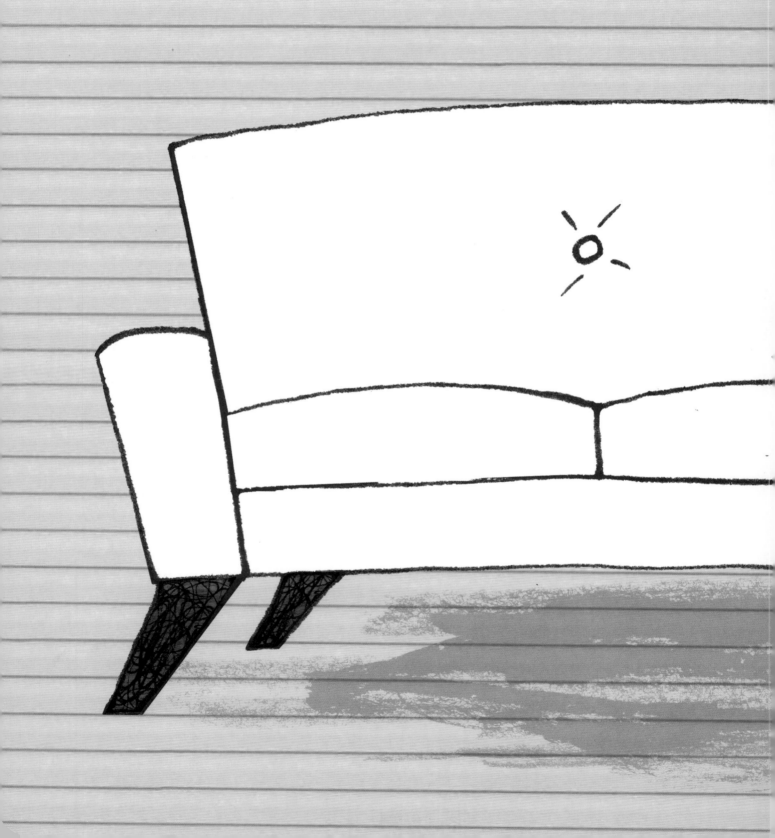

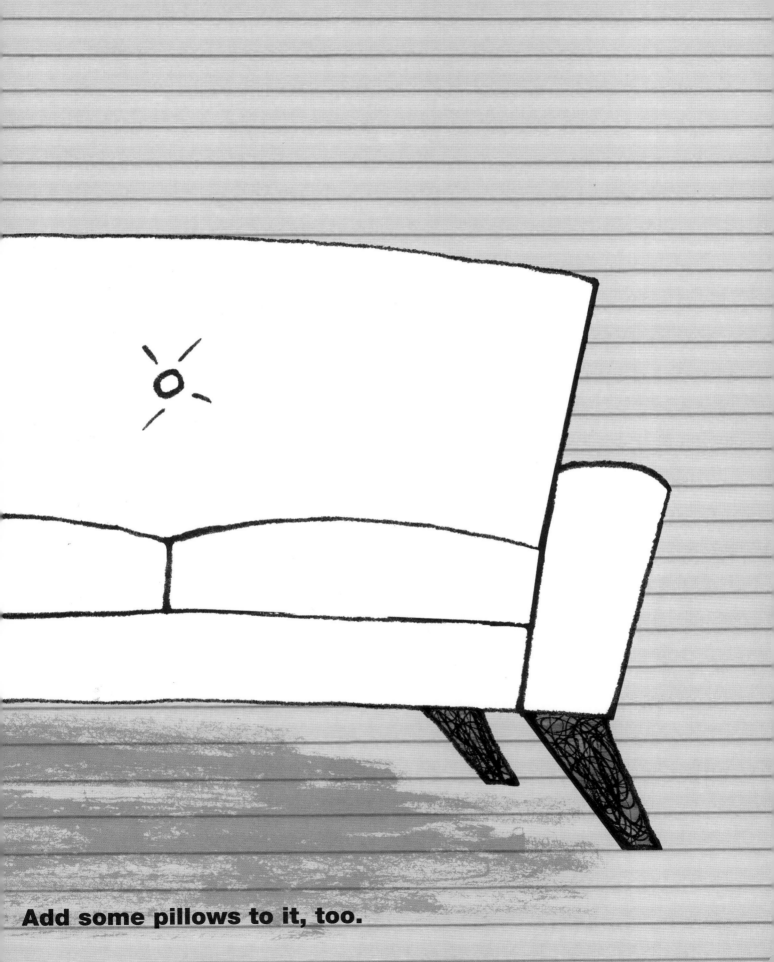

Add some pillows to it, too.

Draw some **caterpillars** in this meadow.

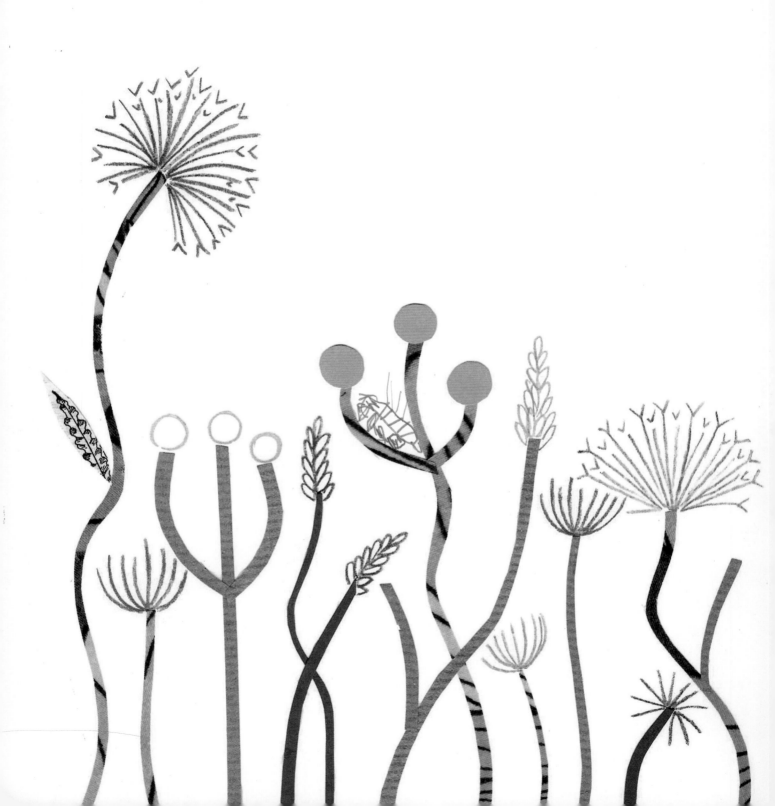

Draw some *butterflies* flying above it.

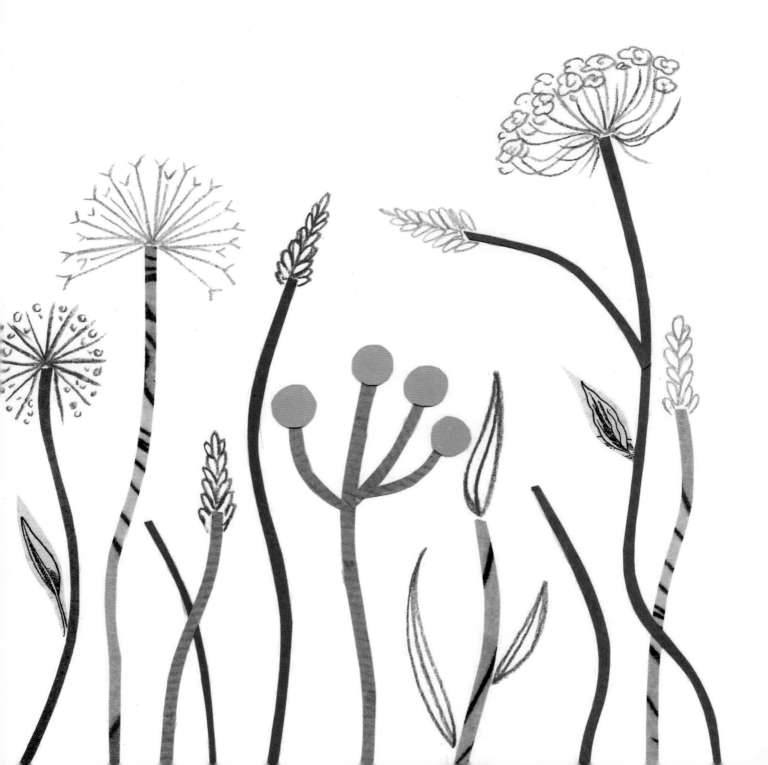

Draw a PERFORMANCE

that is showing on this stage.

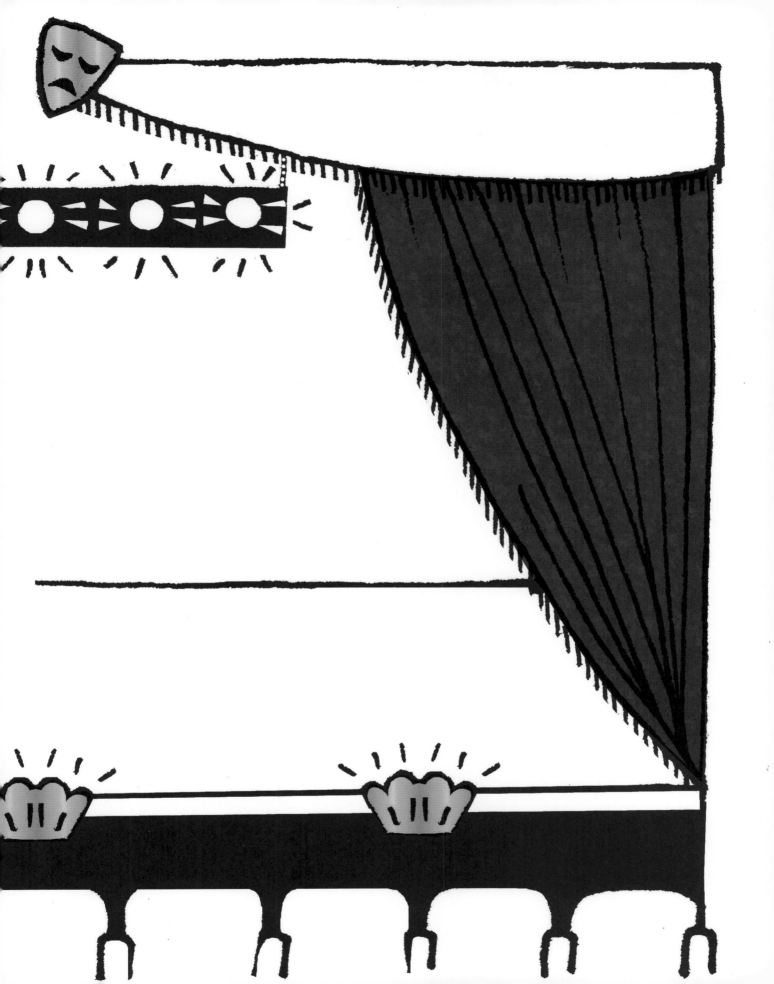

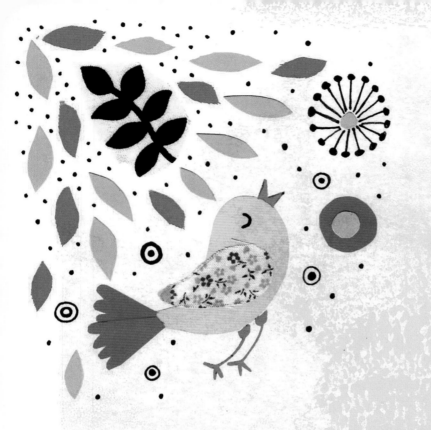

Draw your *mood*
using a single color.

Draw ...
a president,
a baseball player,
and a **clown.**

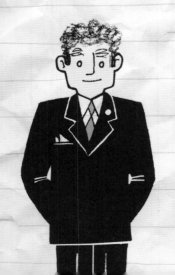
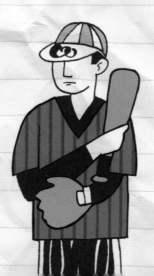
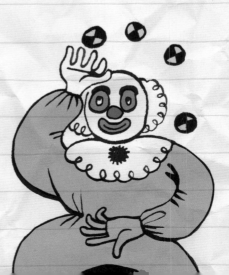

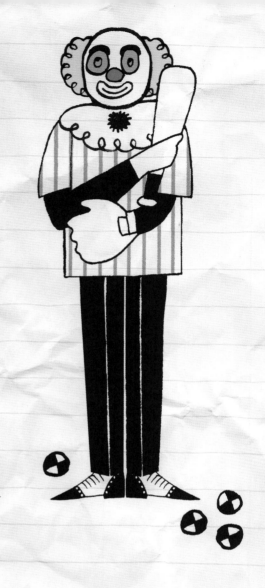

Now draw one image of all three.

Design some

masquerade

masks.

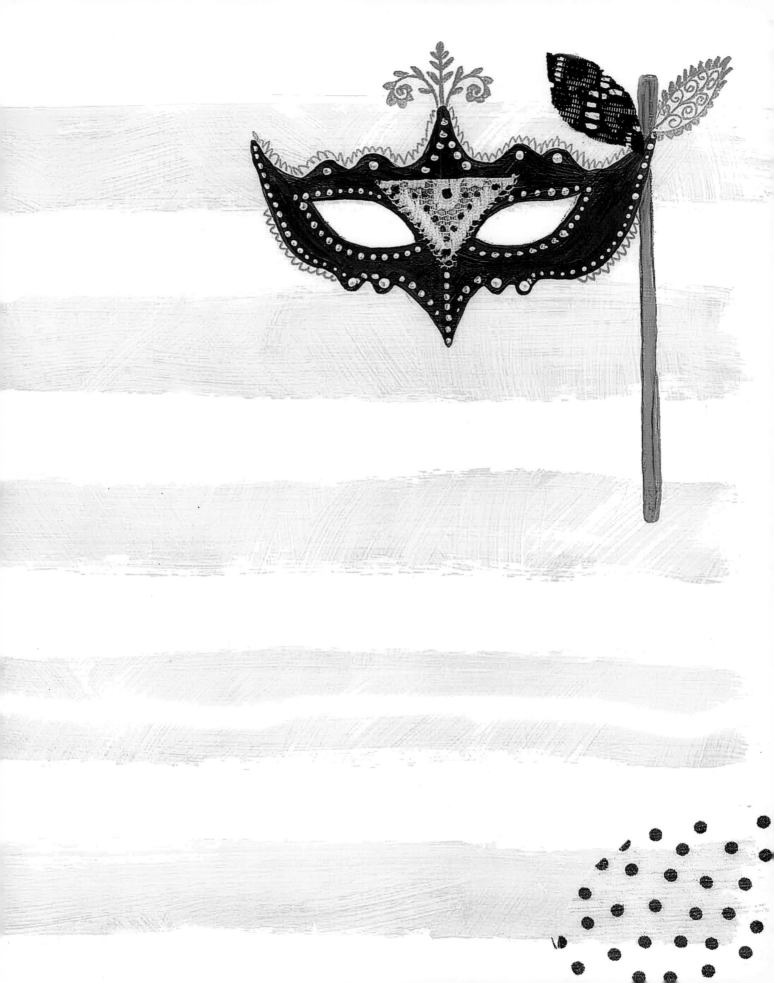

Draw a HORSE
pulling this carriage.

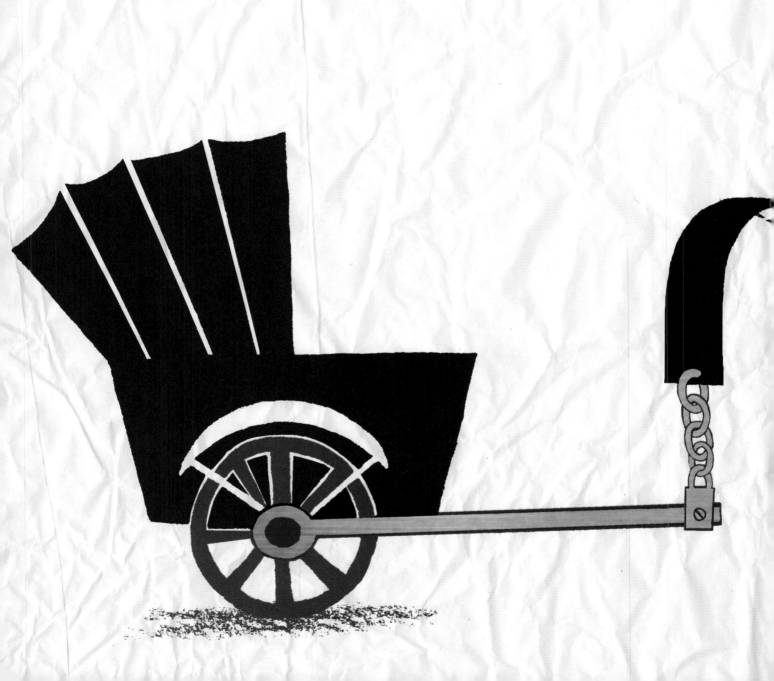

" Every was an am

Ralph Waldo

artist first ateur."

Emerson.

Fill these pages with **RED** creatures.

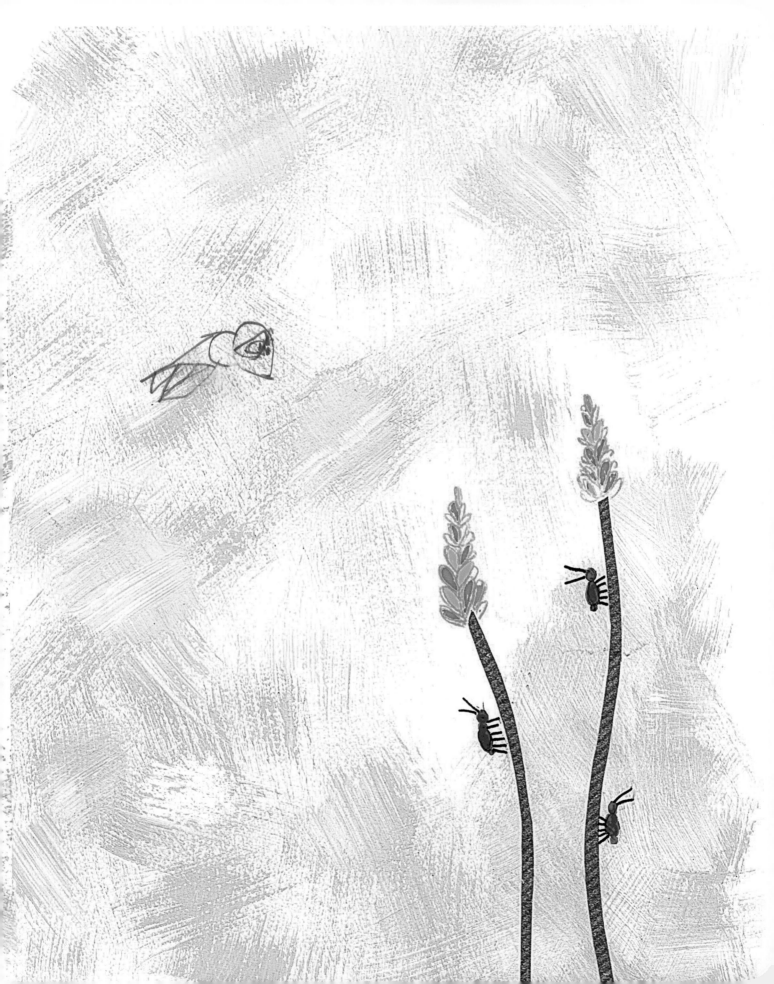

Turn these shapes into
DINOSAURS.

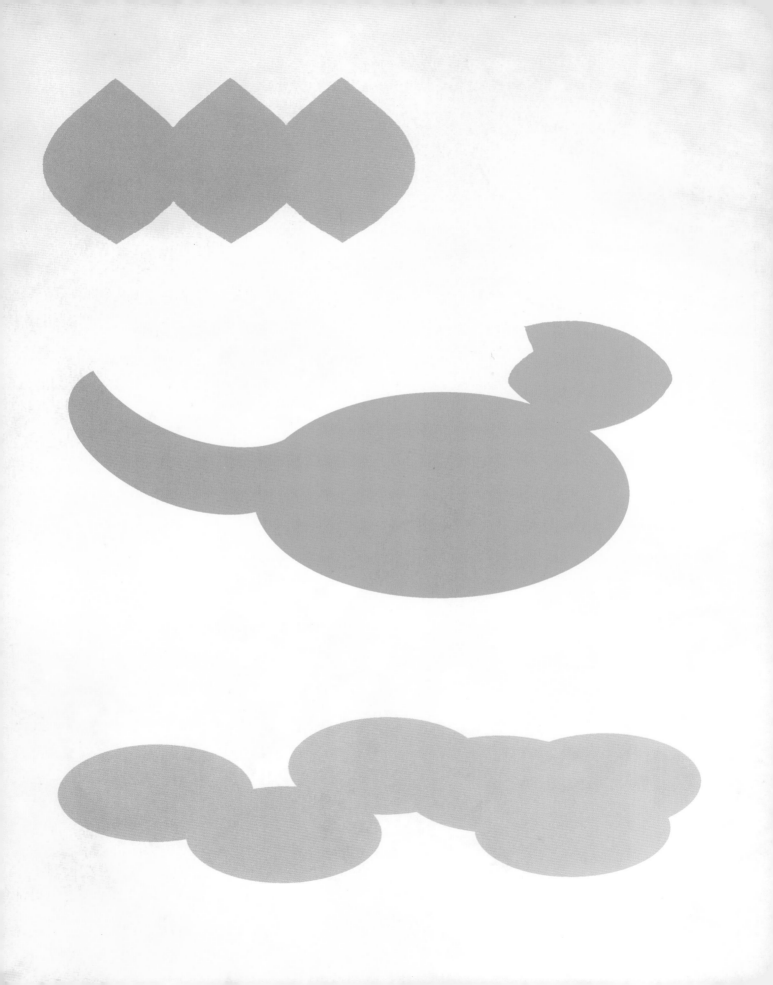

Without taking your *pen off of the page,* draw what is outside your window.

Give these feet a
pedicure.

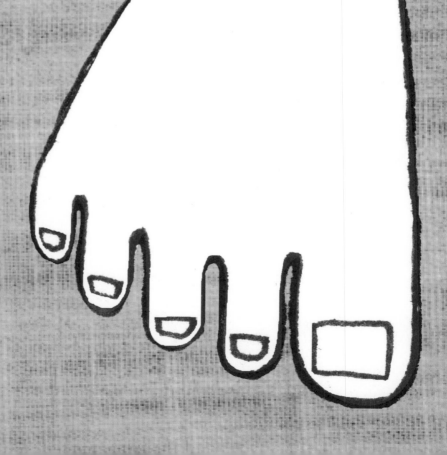

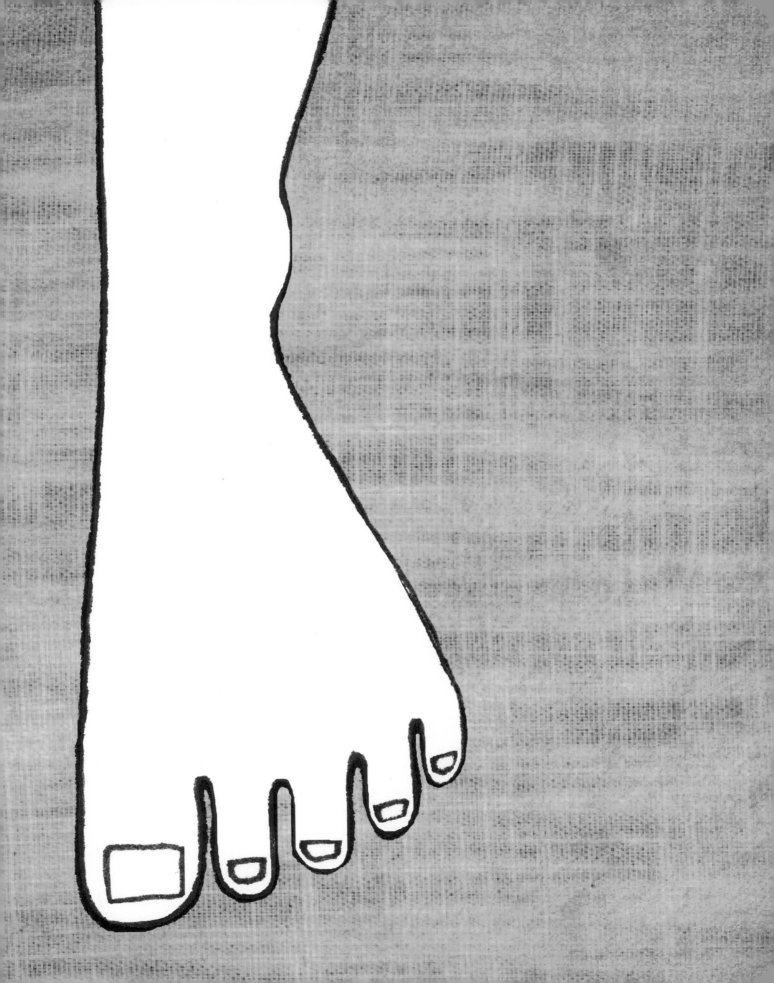

Draw something **DANGEROUS.**

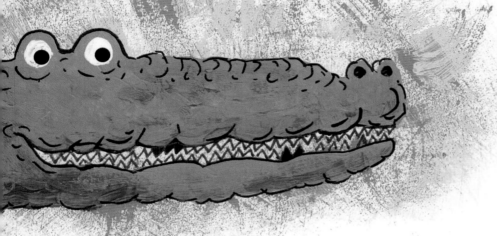

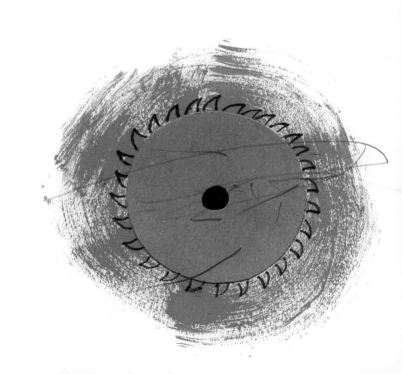

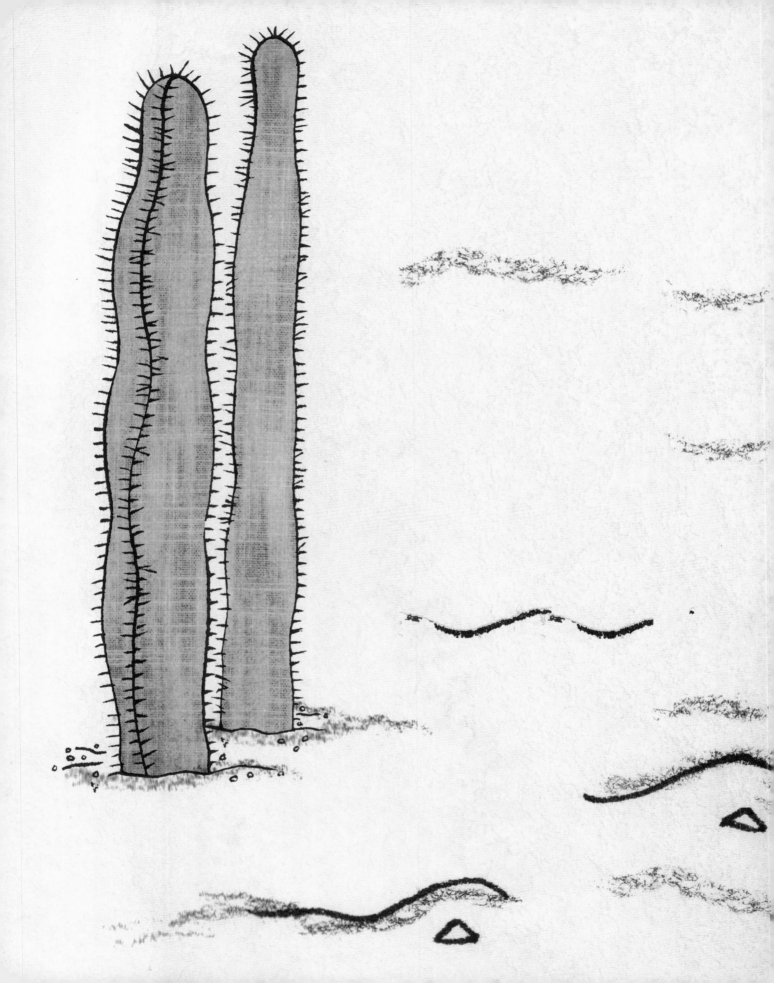

Fill this
desert **with life.**

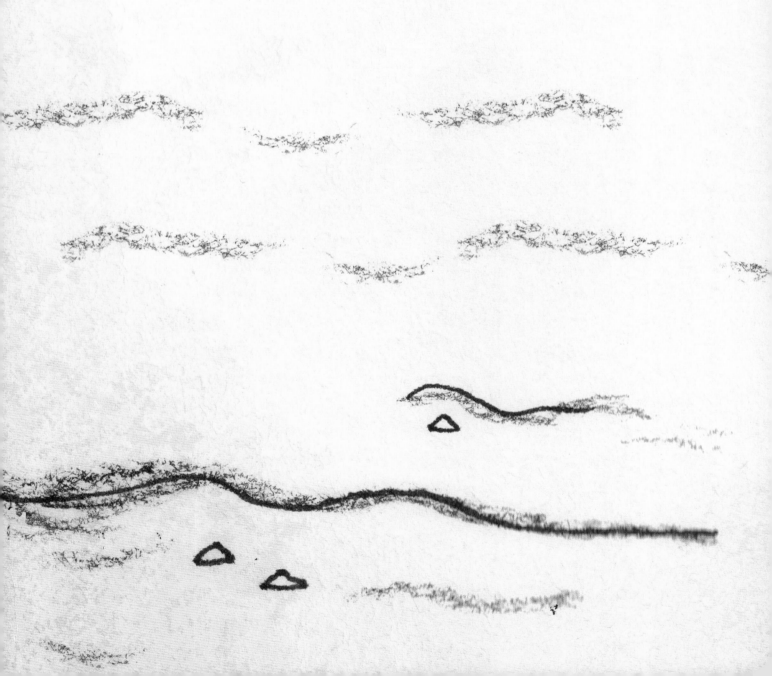

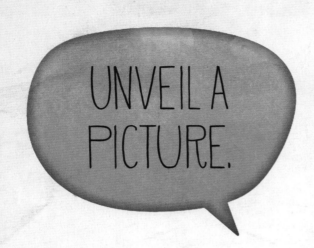

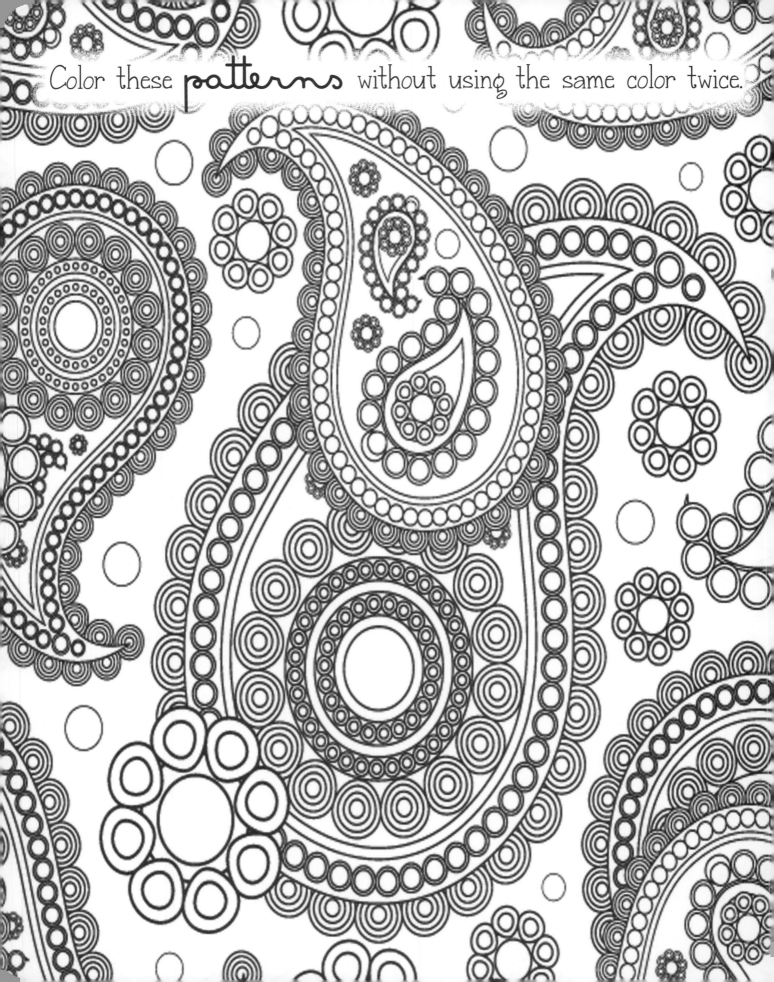

Color these patterns without using the same color twice.

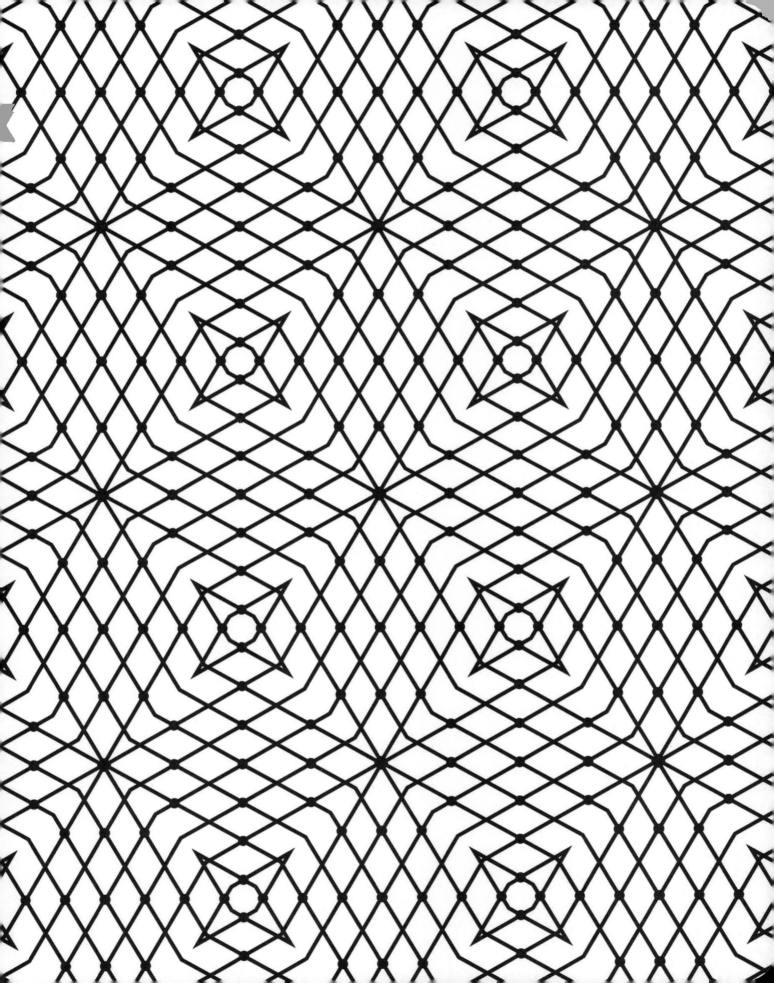

Draw a troupe of

fire - breathing reptiles.

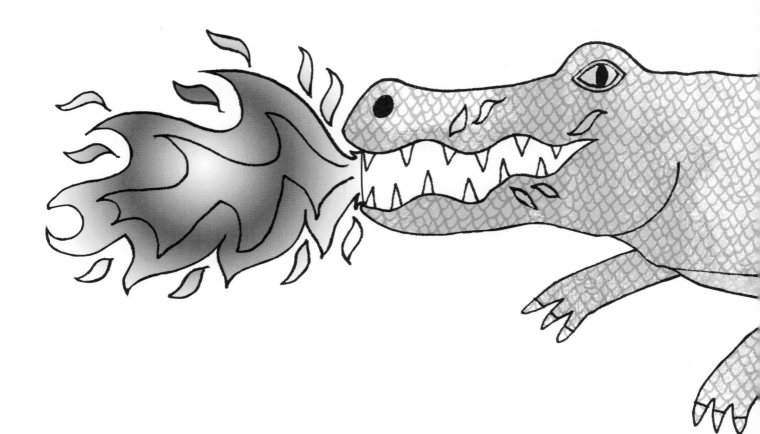

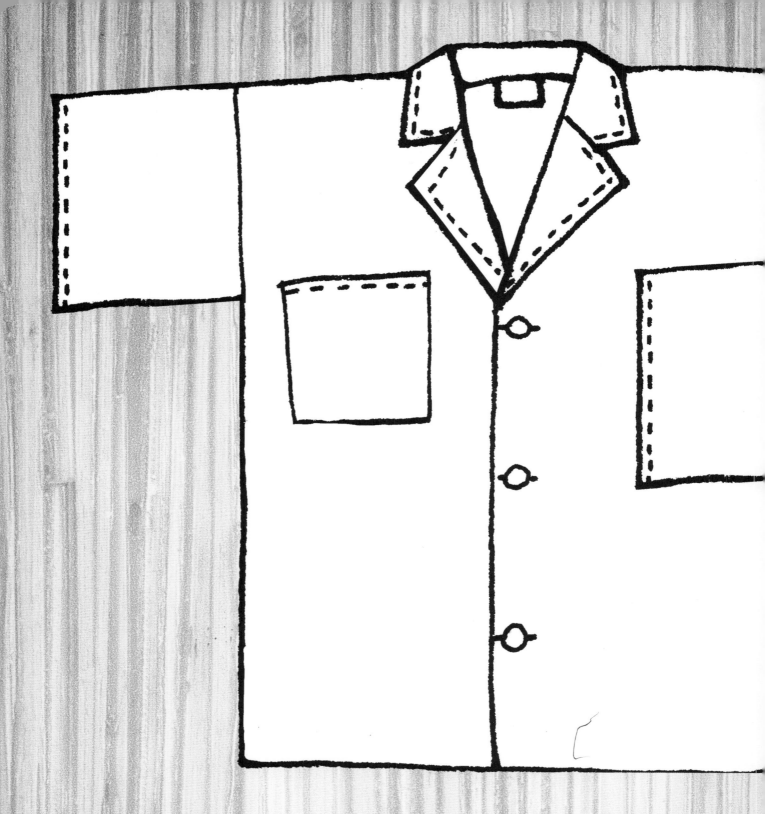

Add bright and colorful designs to these

HAWAIIAN SHIRTS.

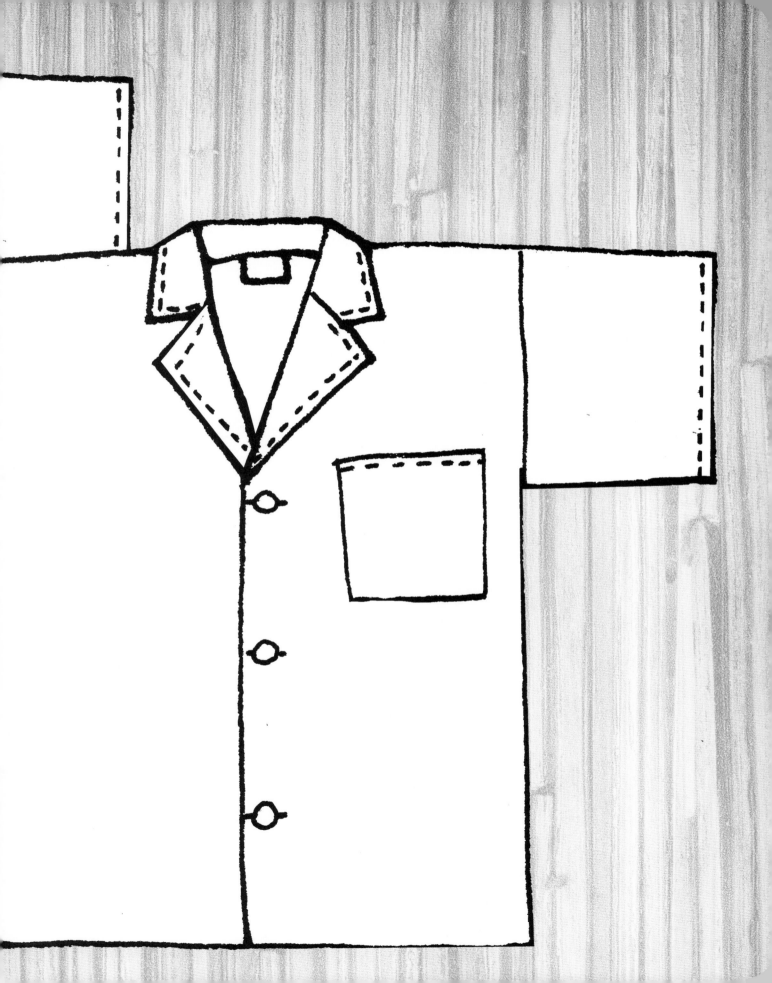

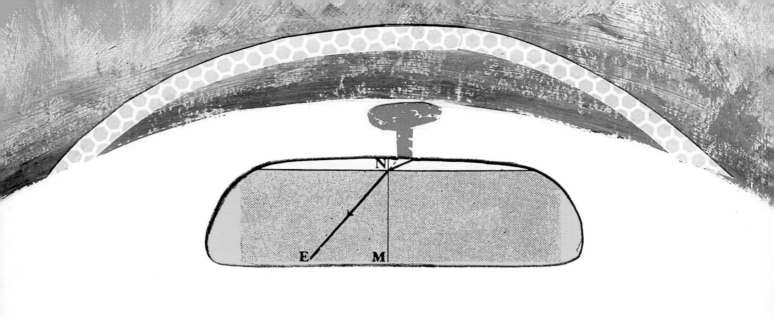

Draw the view from this
car window.

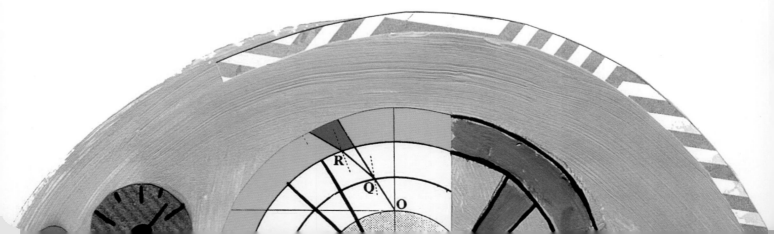

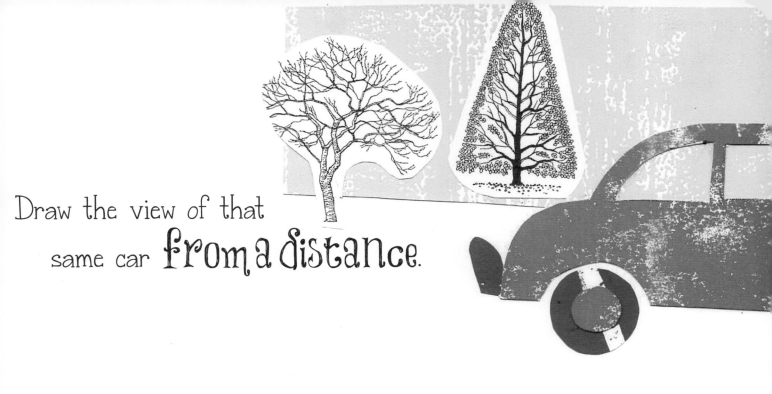

Draw the view of that same car **from a distance.**

Add your
favorite
toppings
to this pizza.

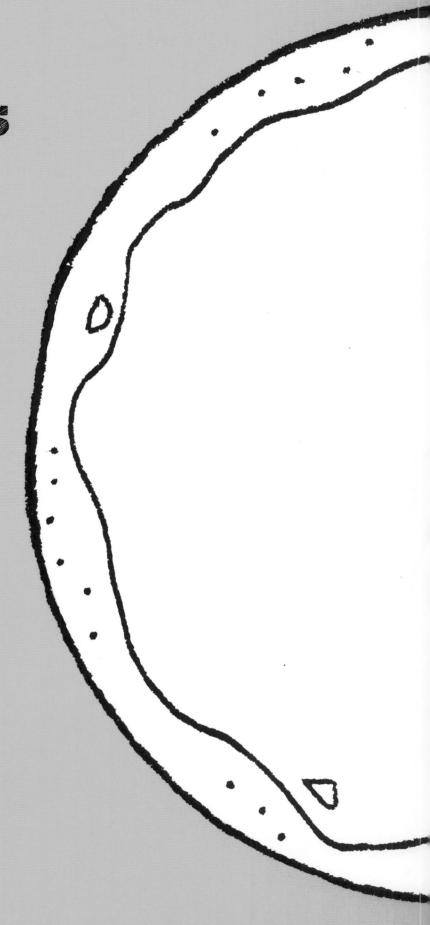

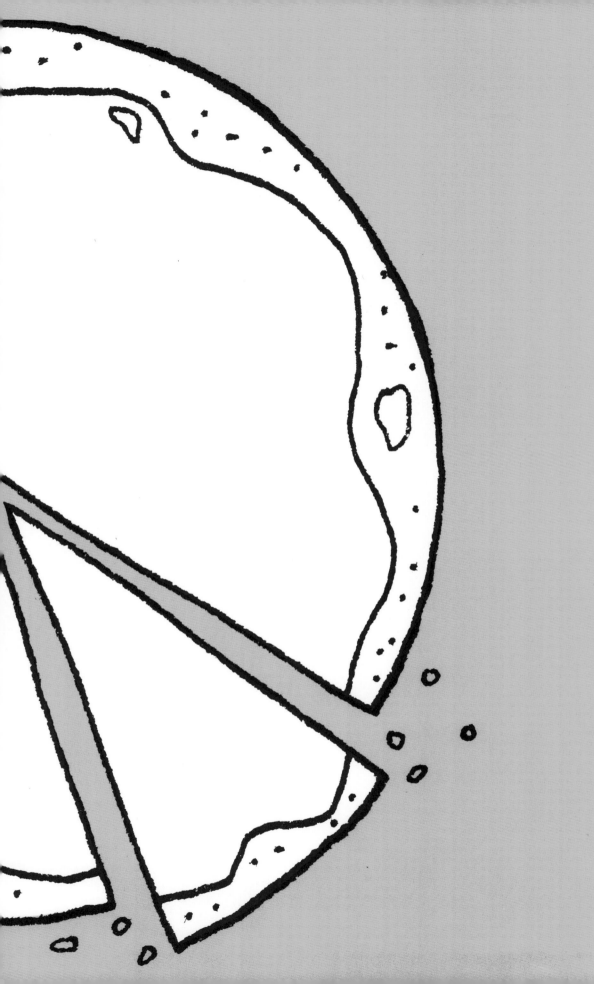

Fill this page with things that SWIM.

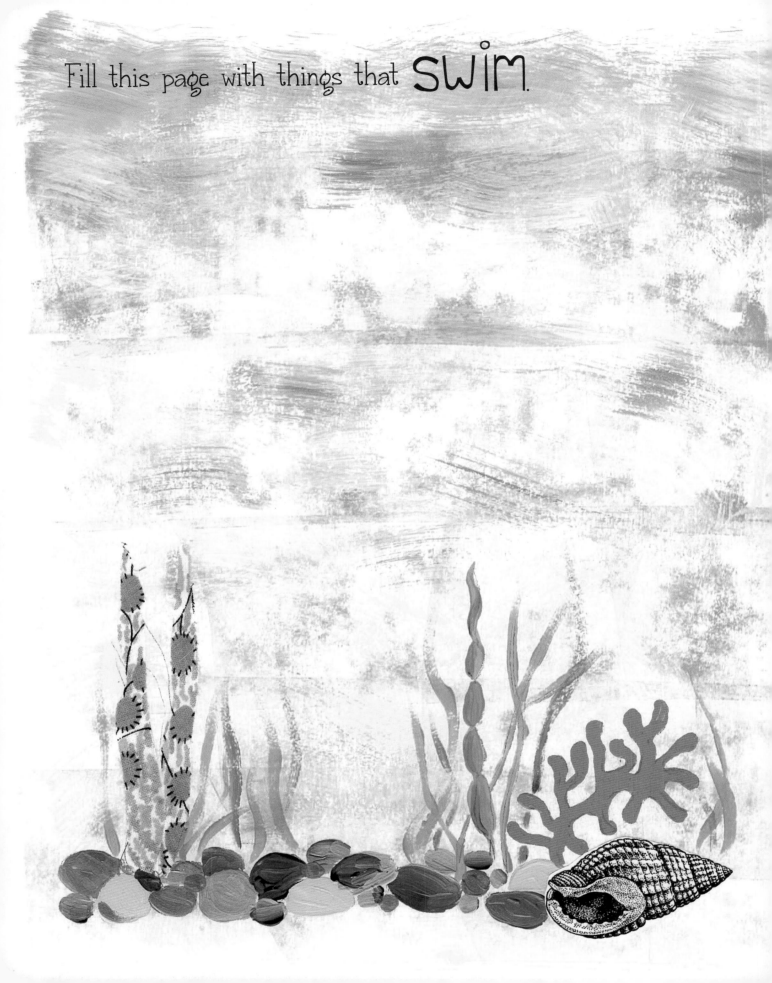

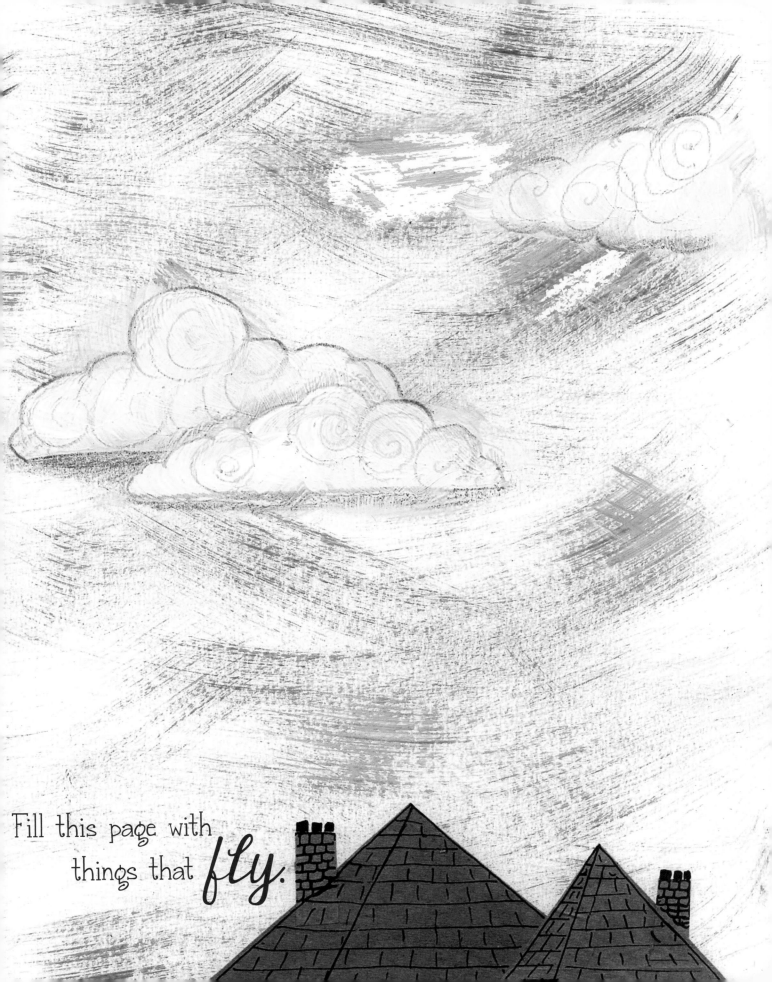

Fill this page with things that *fly.*

Add some **art** to this gallery.

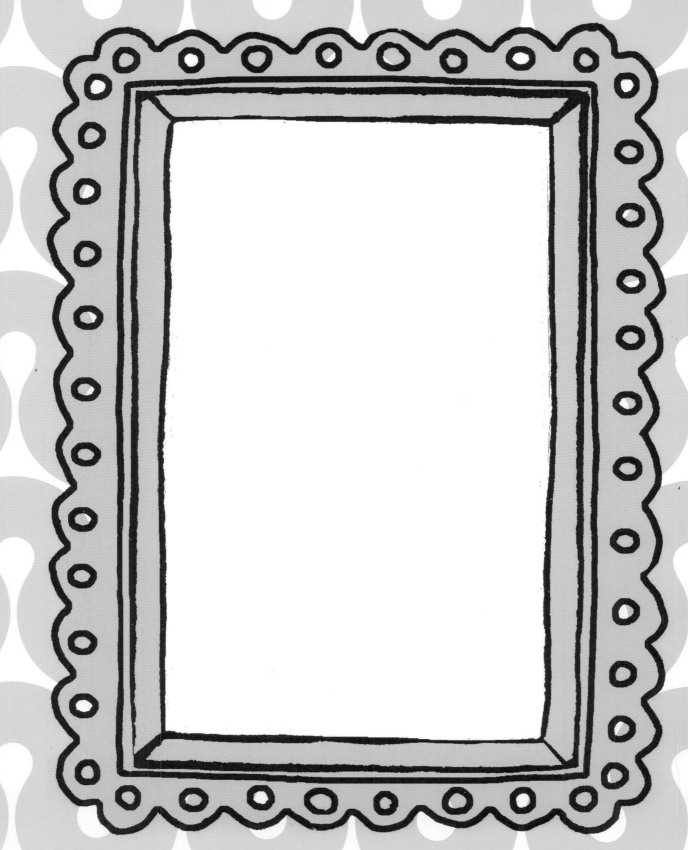

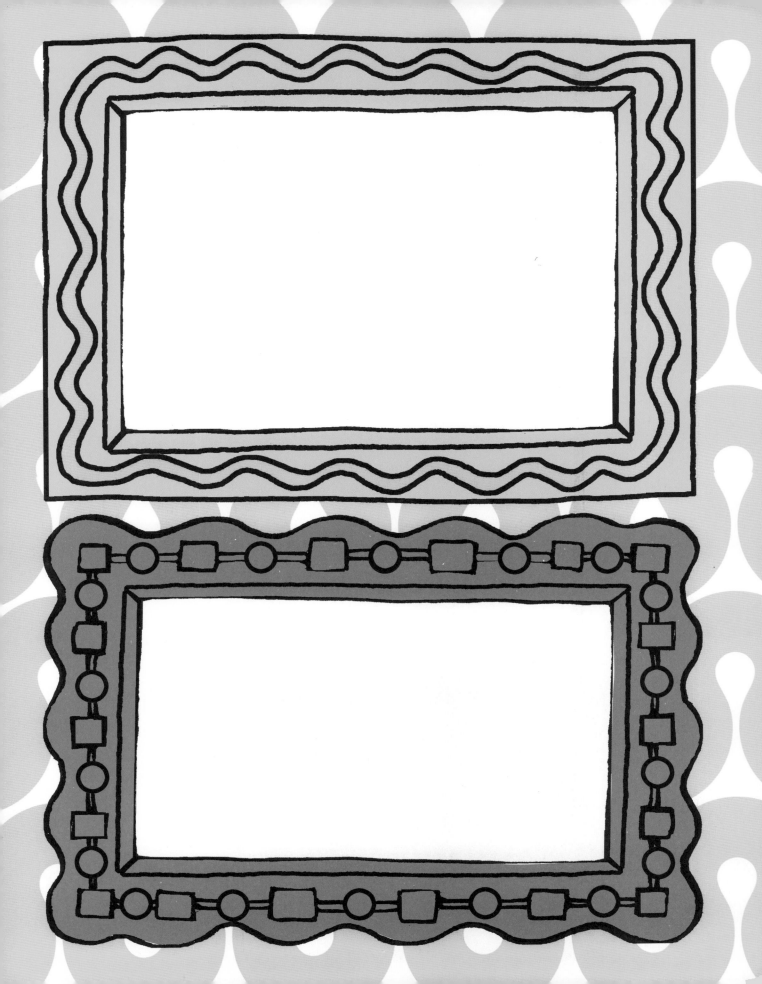

Draw something that is
EXTINCT.

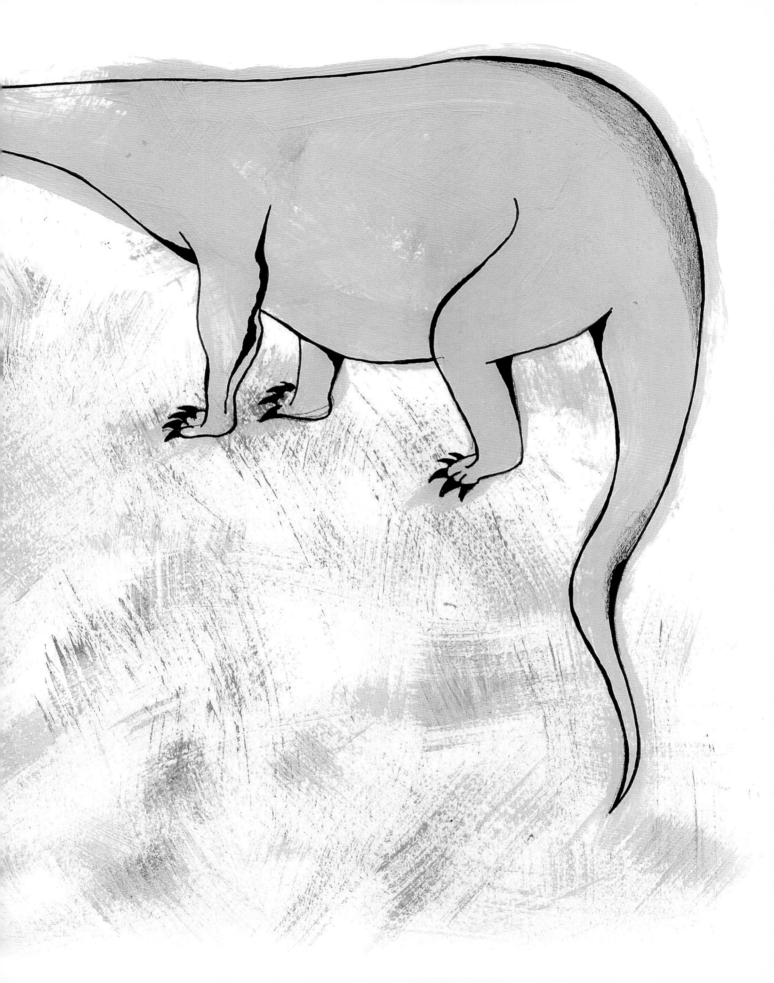

Draw things that can **float** on this lake.

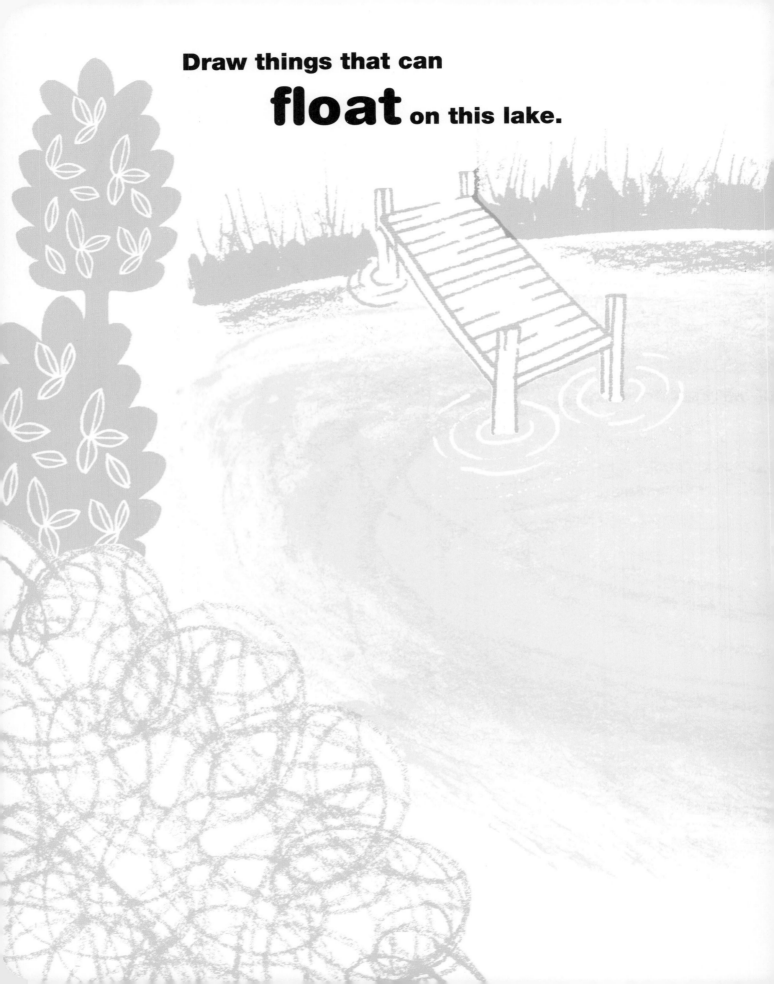

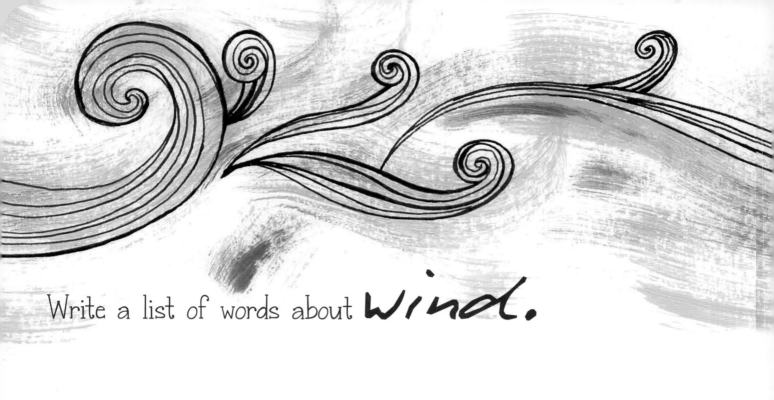

Write a list of words about **wind.**

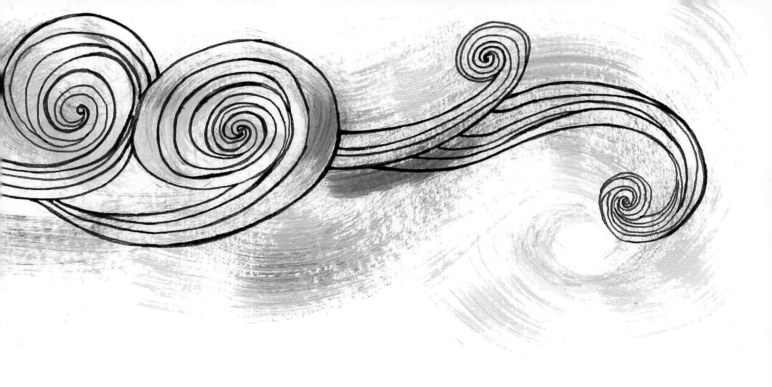

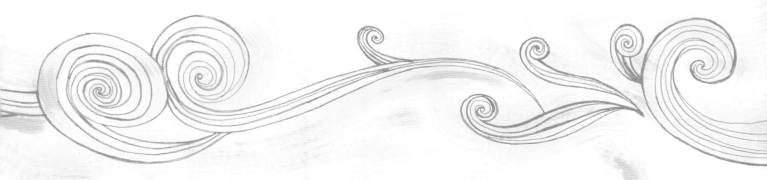

Blow those words into a

drawing of a *windy day.*

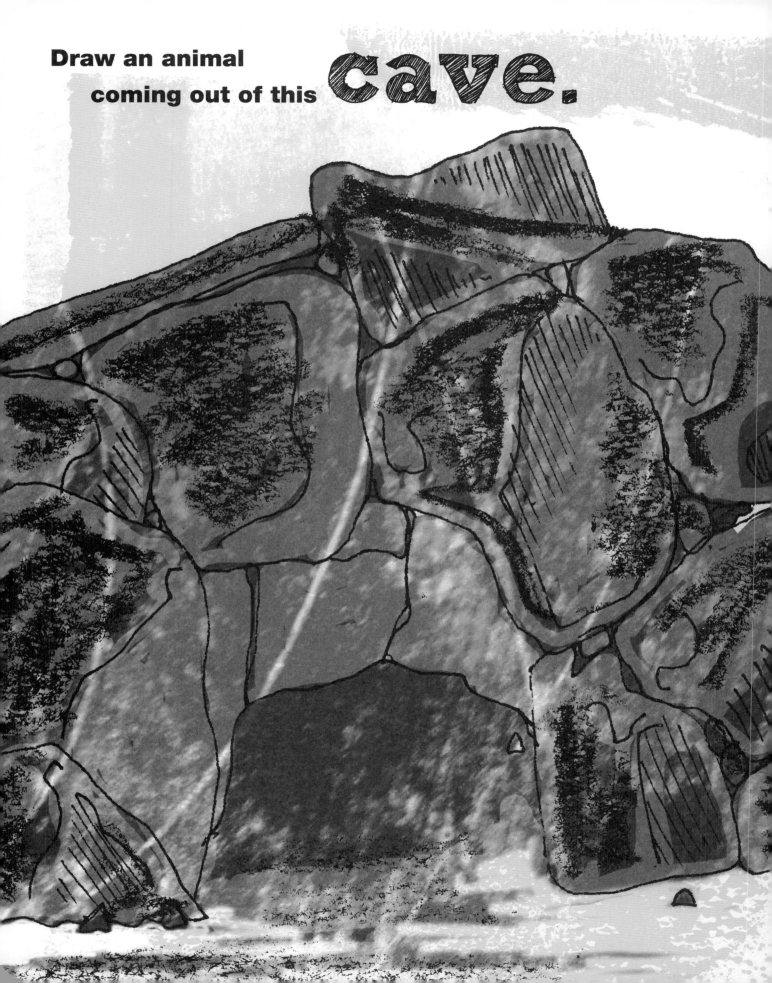

Draw an animal coming out of this cave.

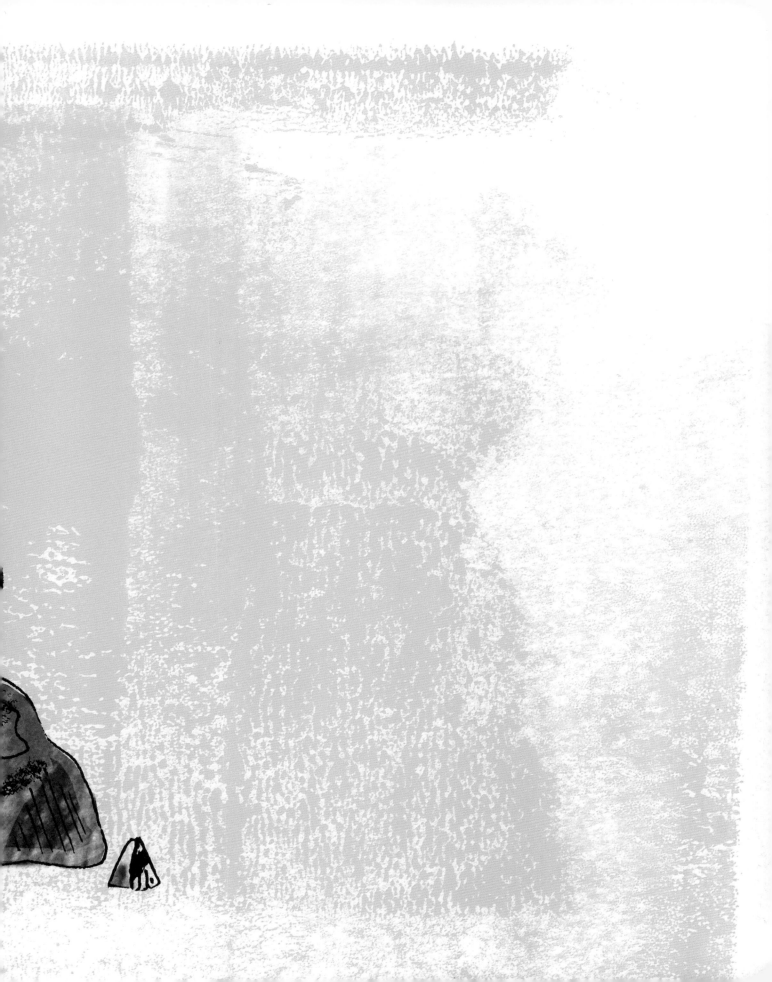

Draw a PREDATOR
chasing its prey.

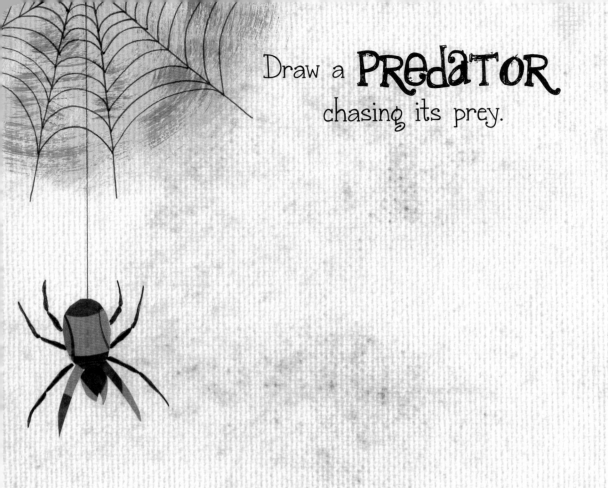

Finish drawing this
castle.

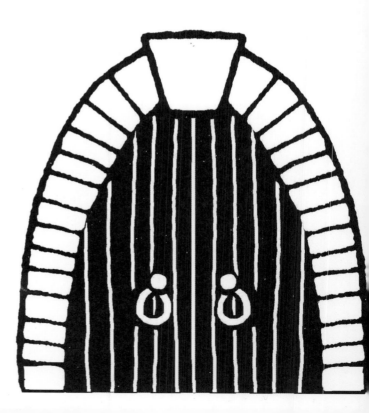

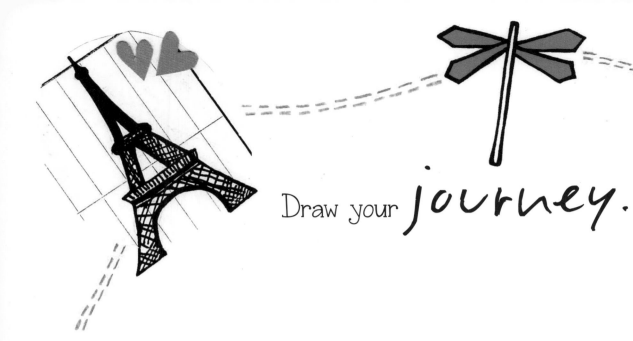

Draw your *journey.*

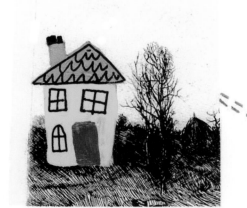

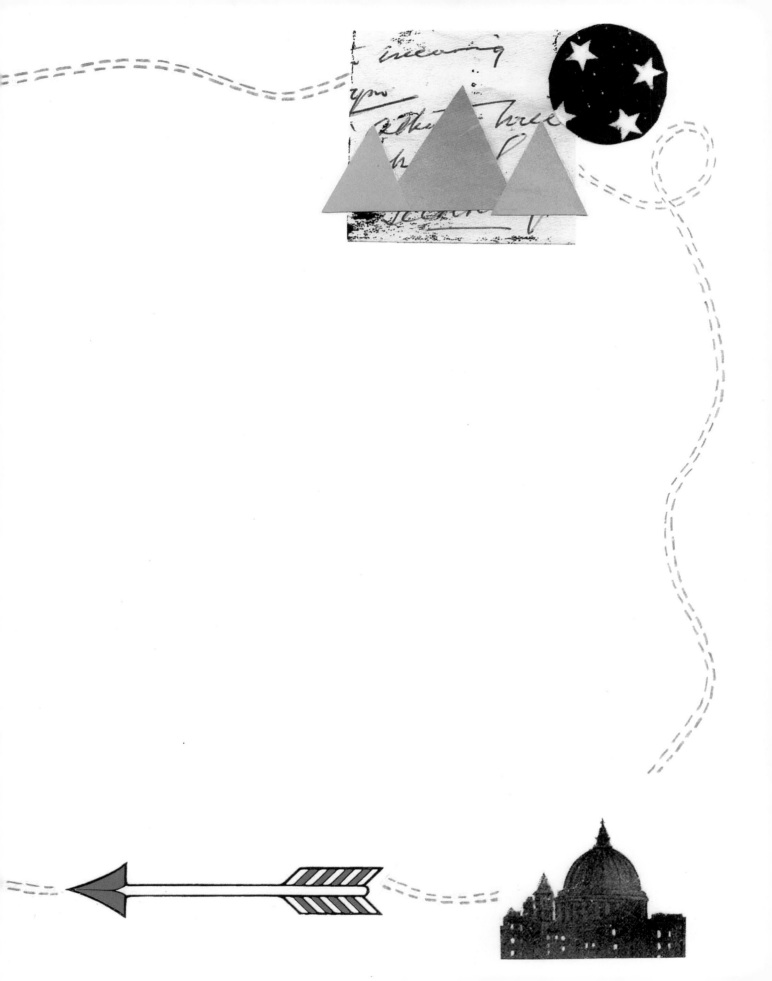

Draw the
passengers
on this bus.

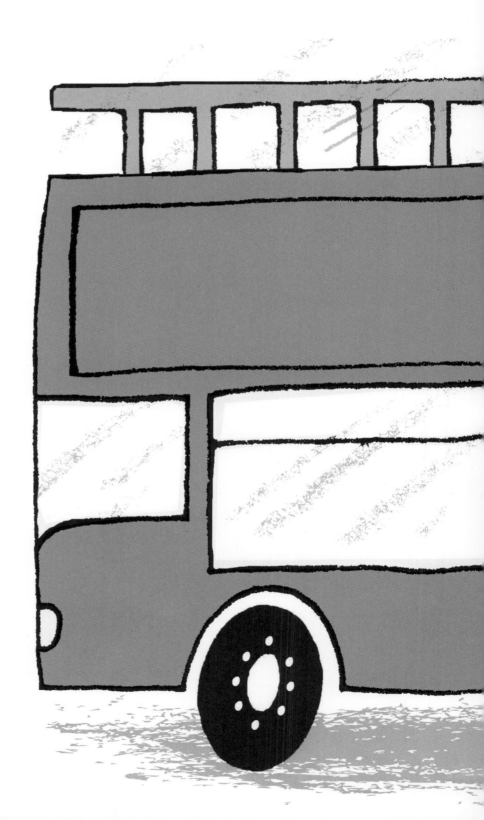

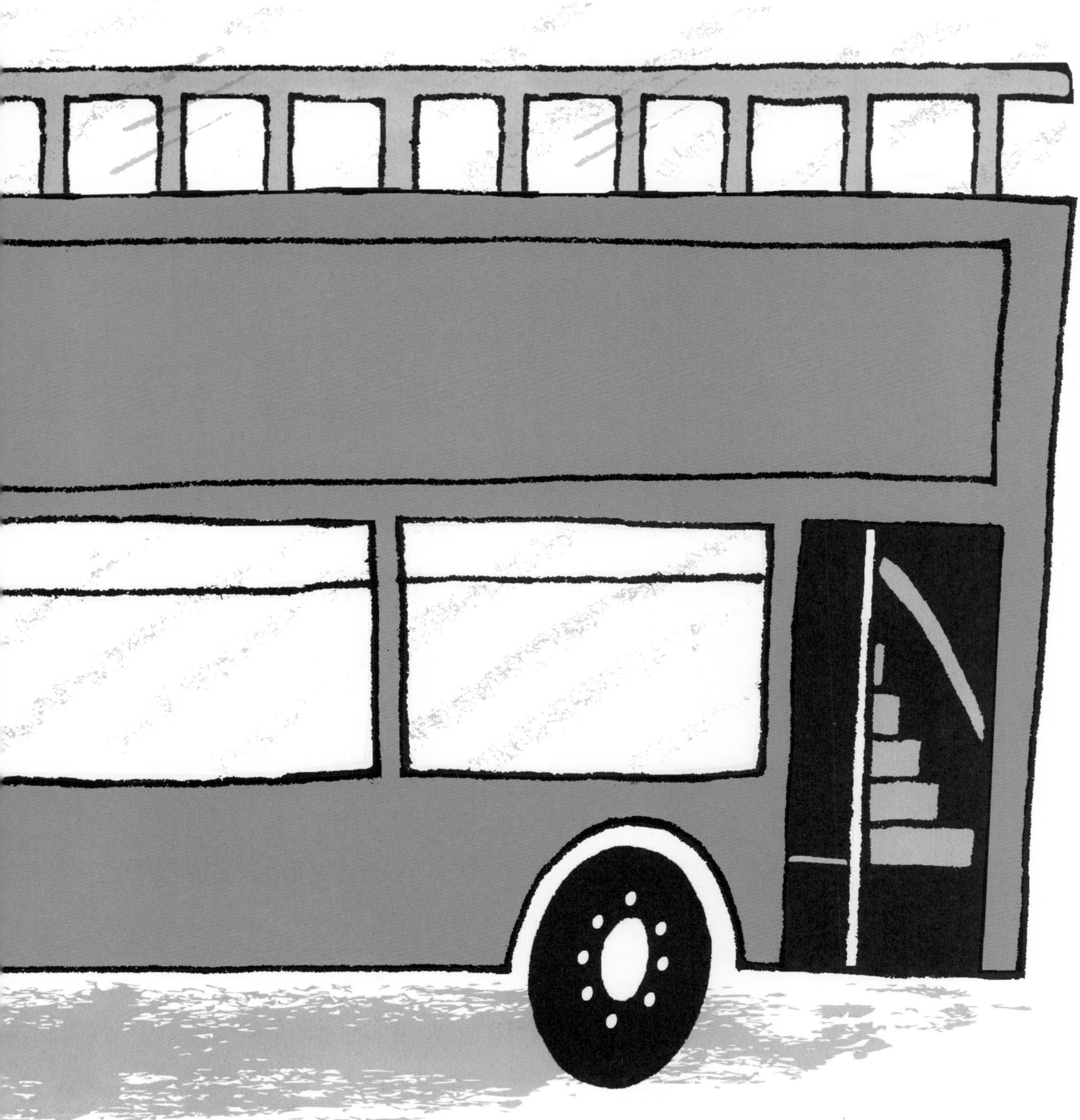

Fill these pages with

COLORFUL STRIPES

to make your own pattern.

Fill this page with **orange** objects.

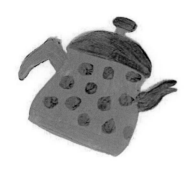

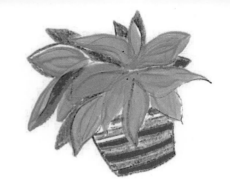

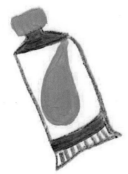

Pick a color.
Look around and draw what you
see that is that color.

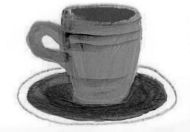

Draw
TRASH OVERFLOWING
into a landfill.

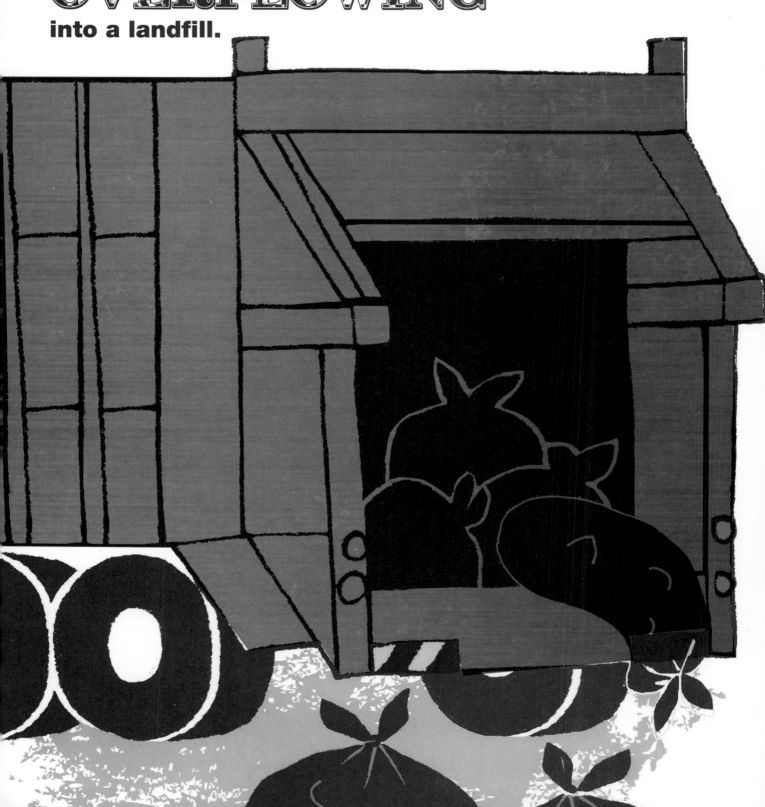

Don't think,
just draw.

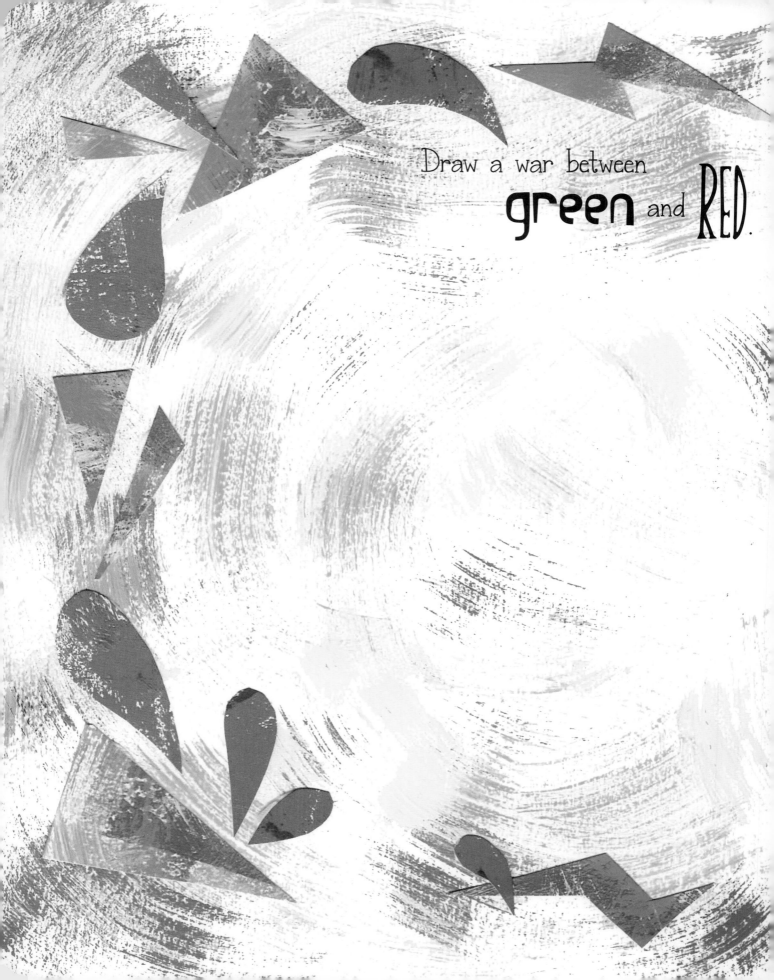

Draw a war between
green and **RED**.

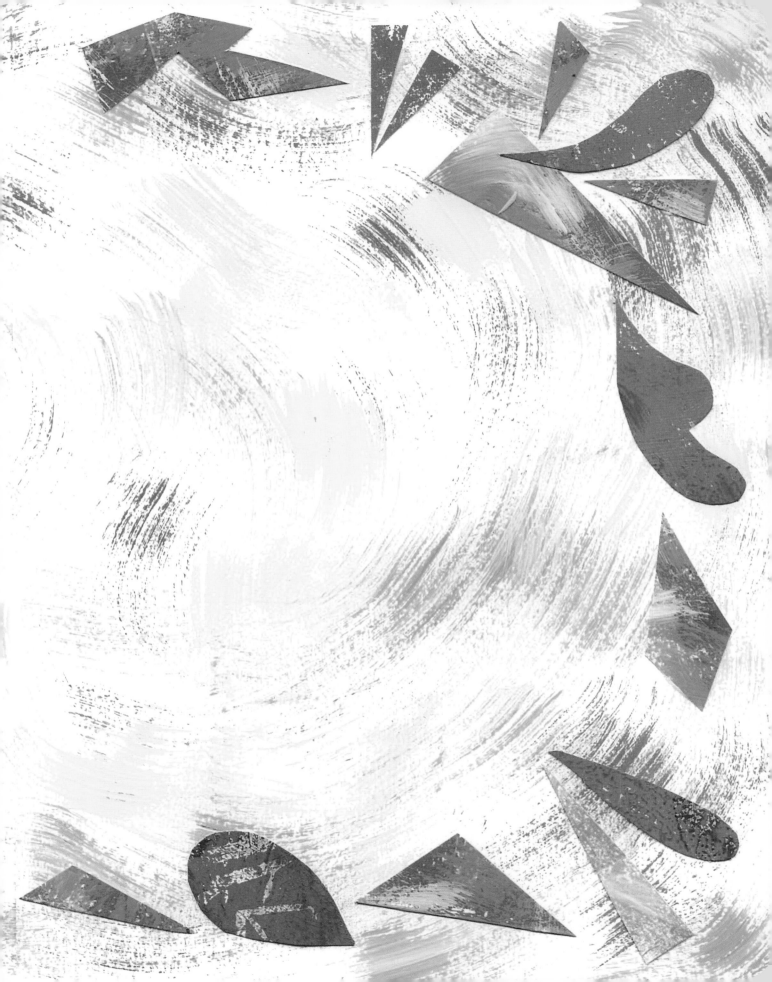

Fill this skyline with

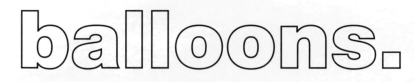

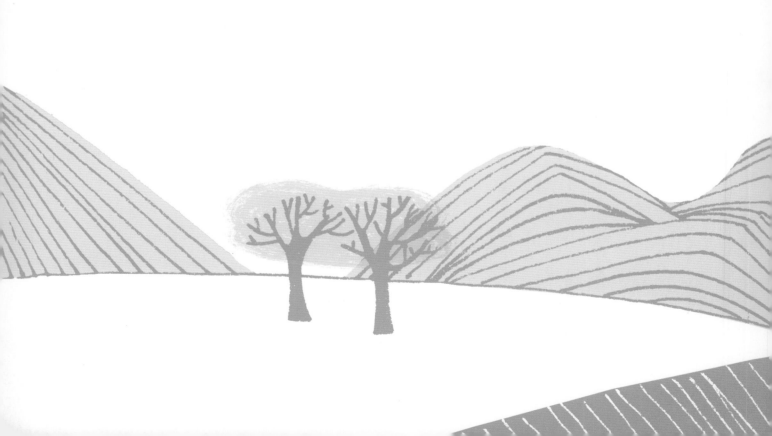

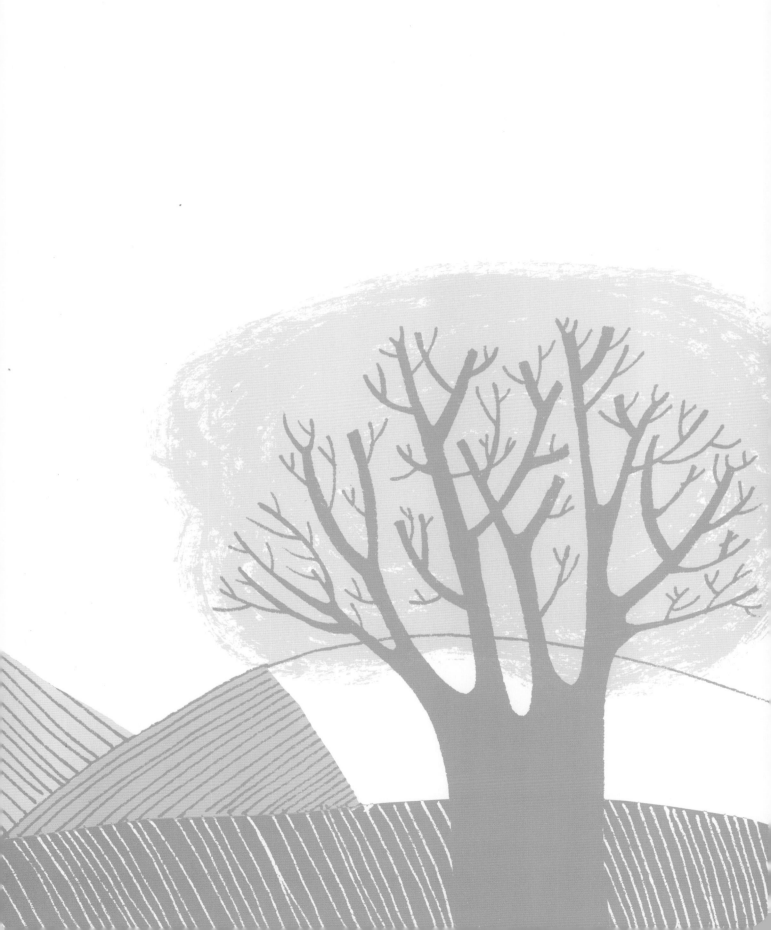

Draw your favorite

AMUSEMENT PARK RIDES.

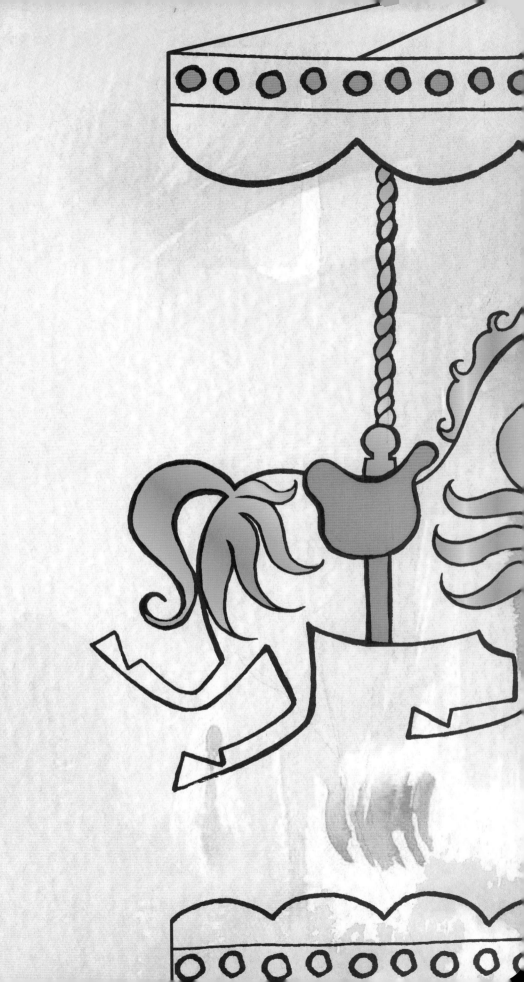

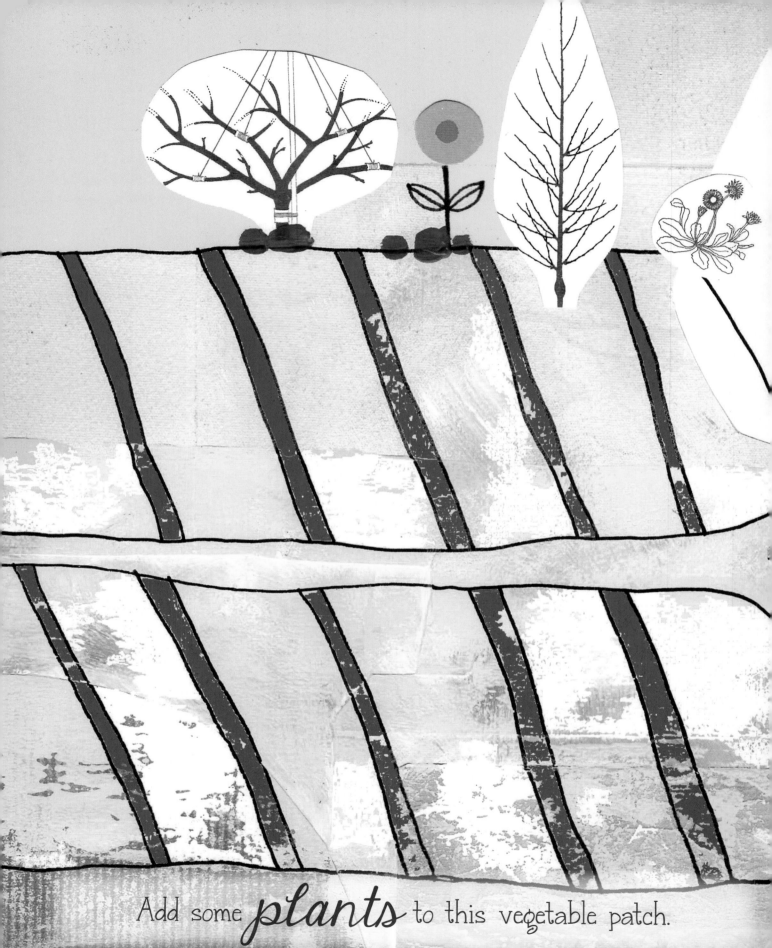

Add some *plants* to this vegetable patch.

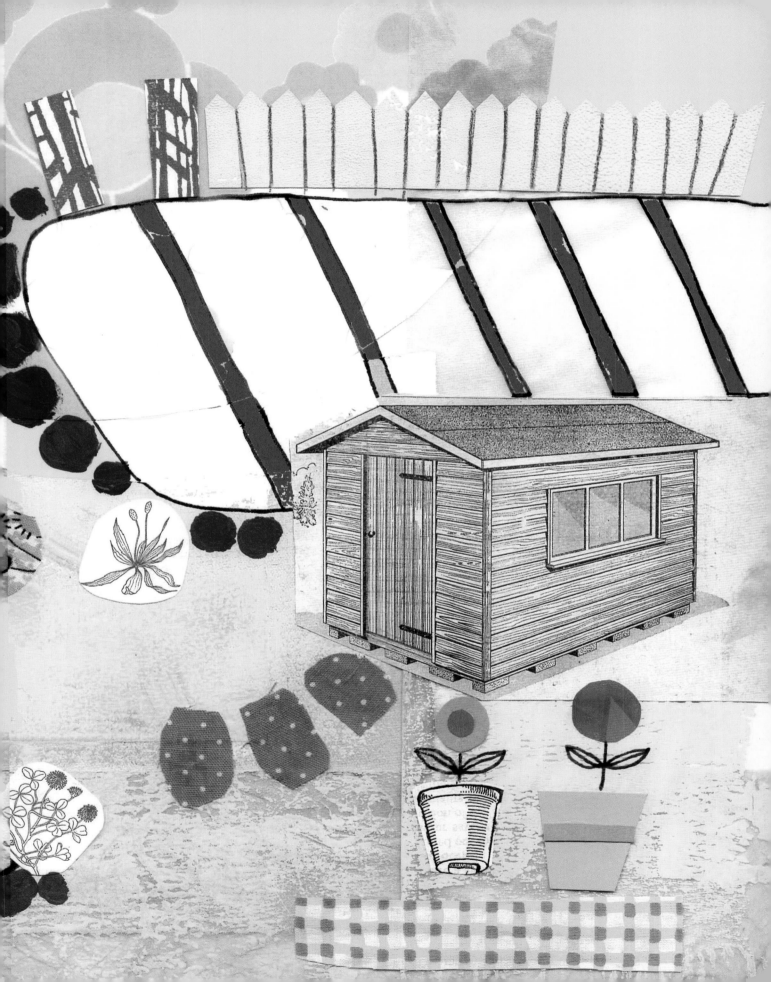

"A #2 PENCIL AND A DREAM

Joyce Meyer.

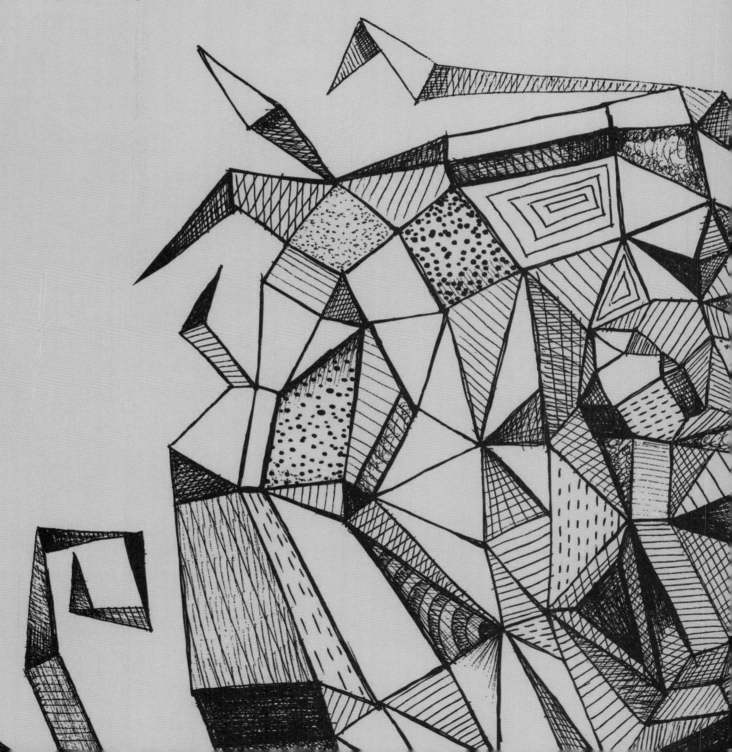

CAN TAKE YOU ANYWHERE."

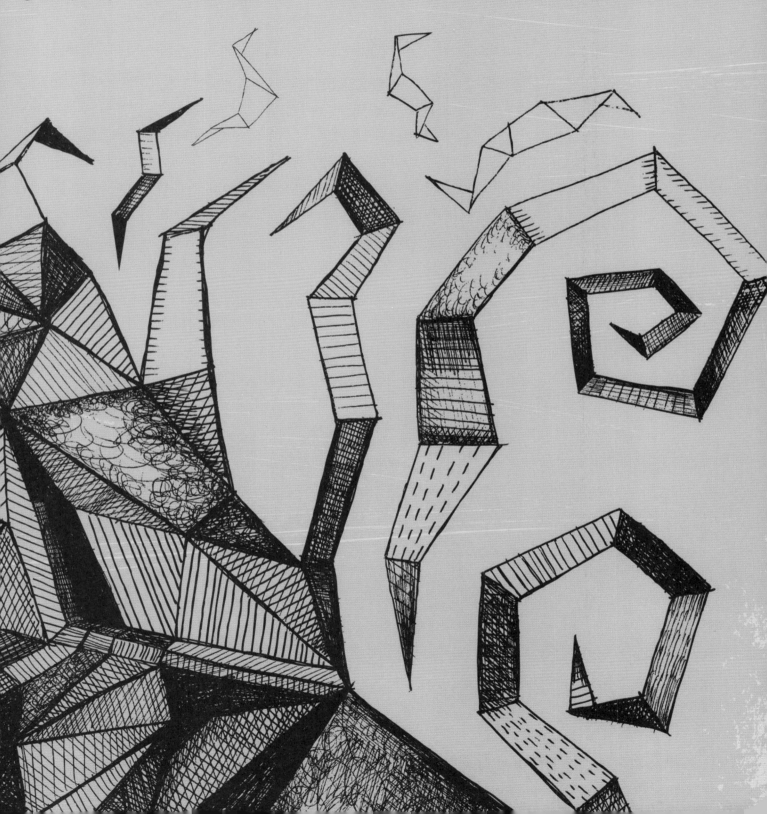

Draw loot spilling from this

treasure chest.

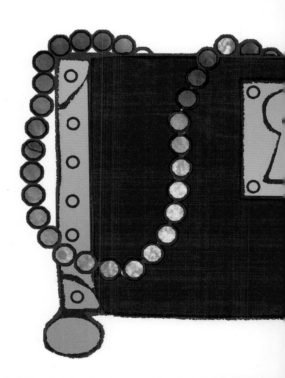

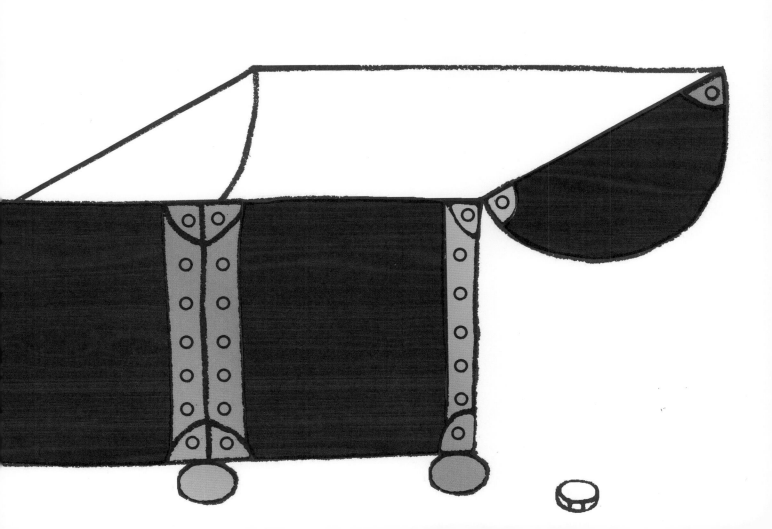

Draw squares *spiraling.*

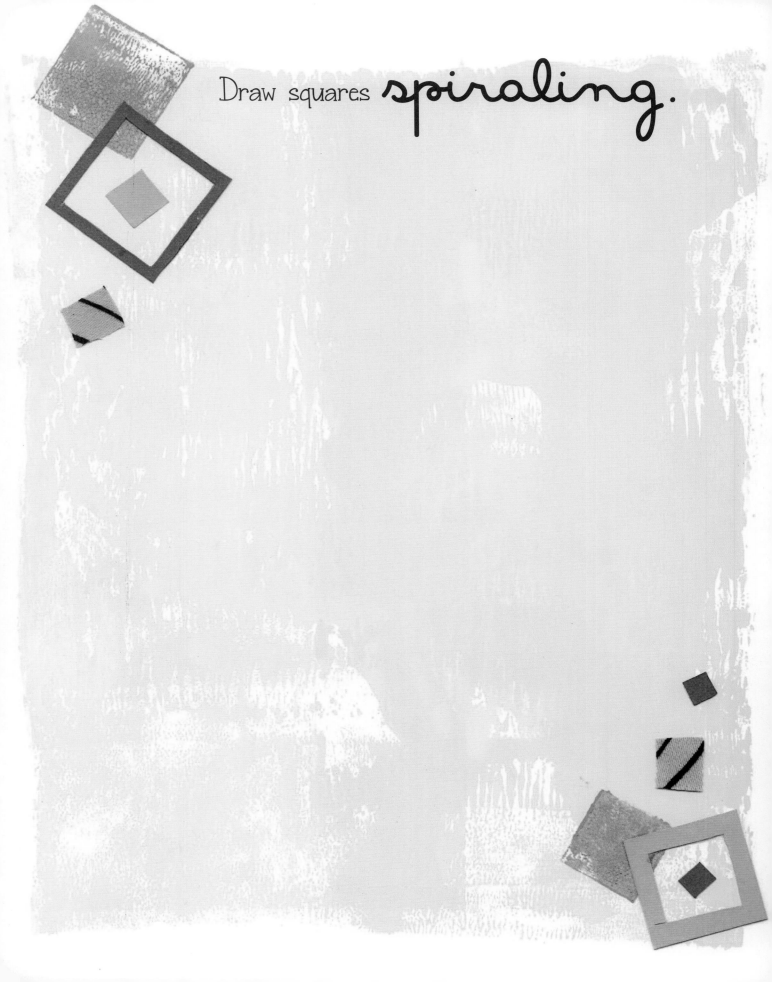

Draw hearts
spinning.

Draw a
cat swimming ...

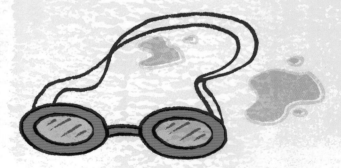

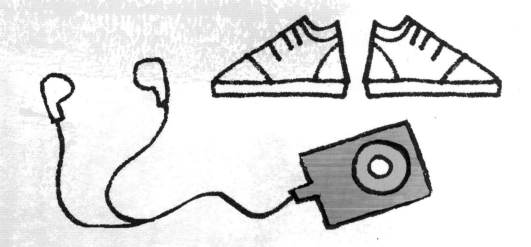

... and a
bird jogging.

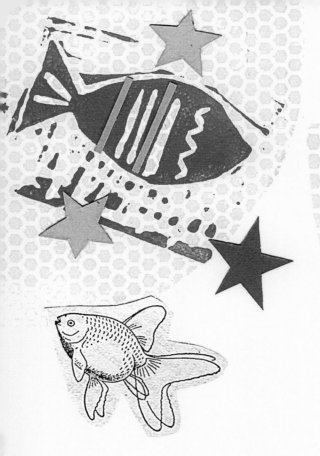

Draw a **DREAM.**

Draw **half of your face** on one side of the circle ...

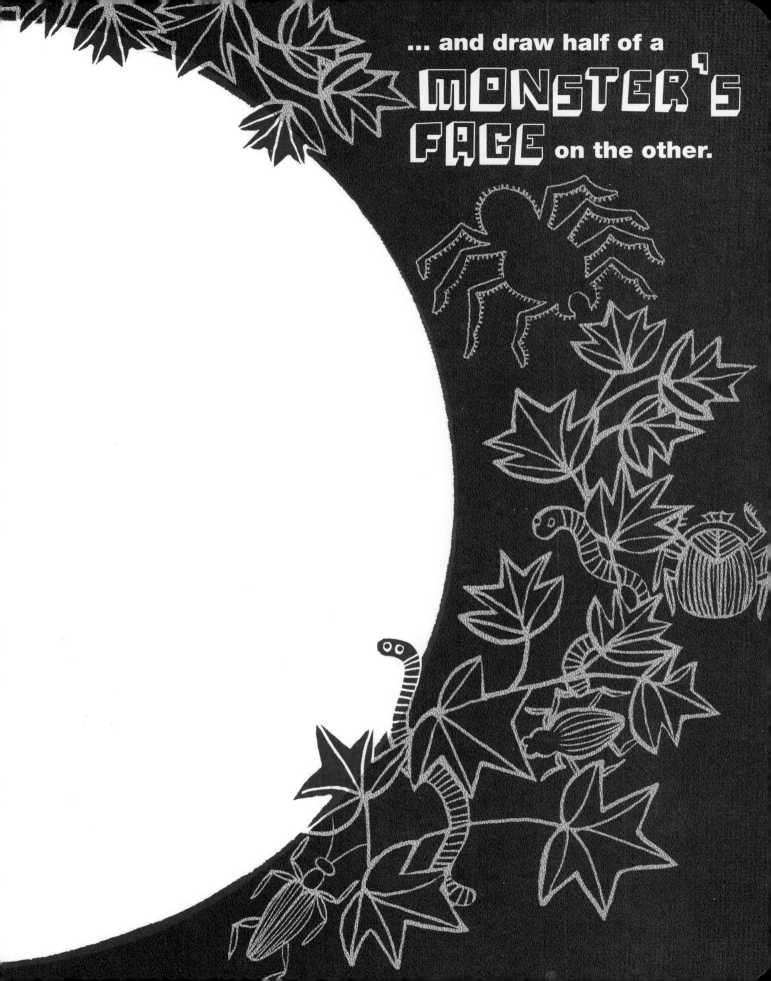

... and draw half of a **MONSTER'S FACE** on the other.

Draw an *animal* from the zoo behind these bars.

Draw the same animal in its
natural habitat.

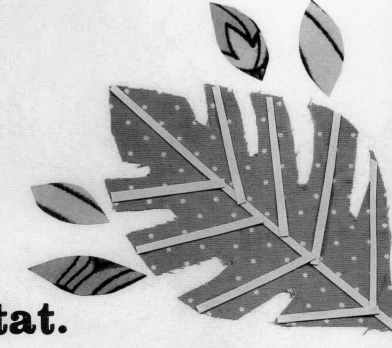

Draw your favorite animal.

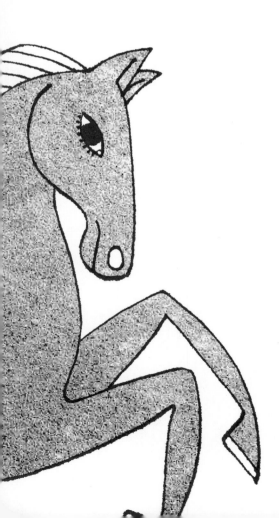

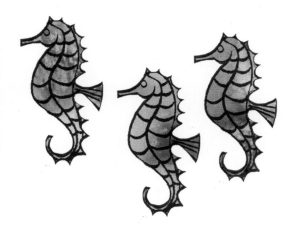

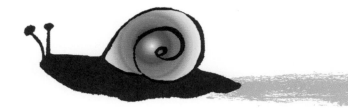

Draw your least favorite animal.

Draw what's
CREEPING
around in the dark.

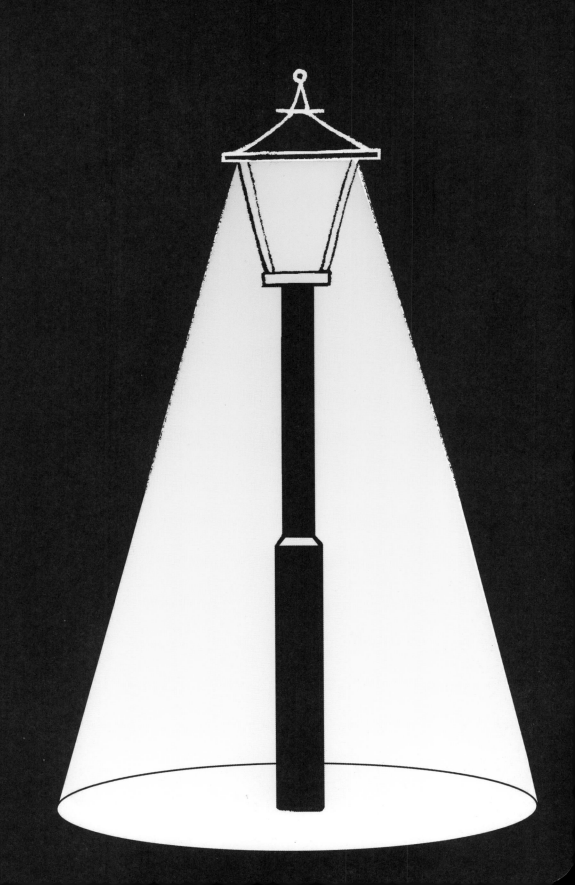

Draw a LandsLide.

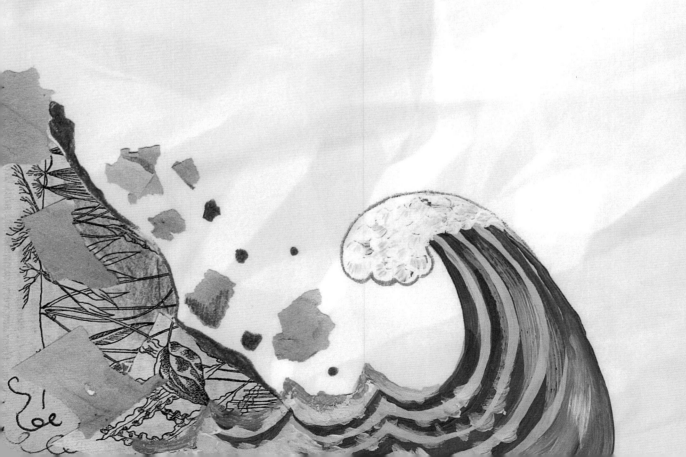

WRAP UP
this boy and girl up for winter.

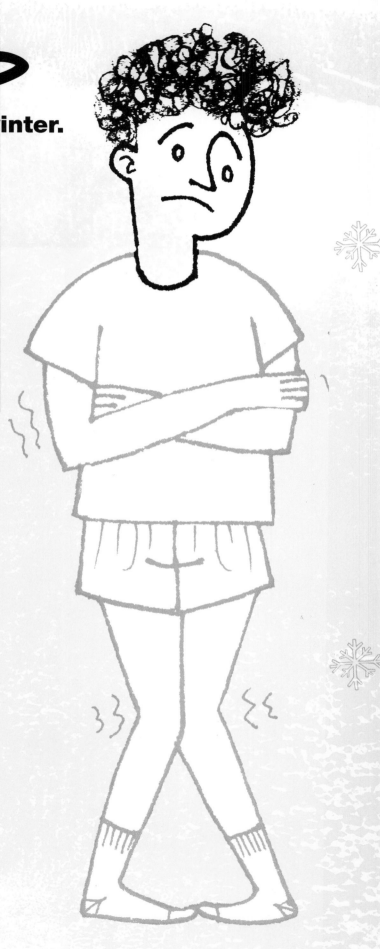

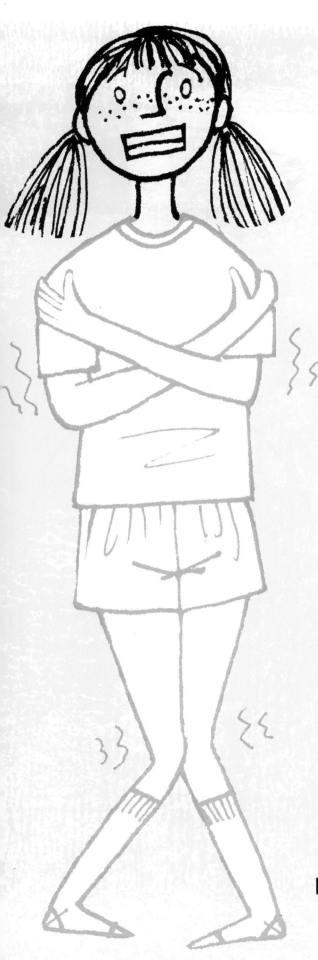

It's snowing, do they need coats, hats, scarfs, and gloves?

Draw the reflection in a ...

SPOON,

doorknob,

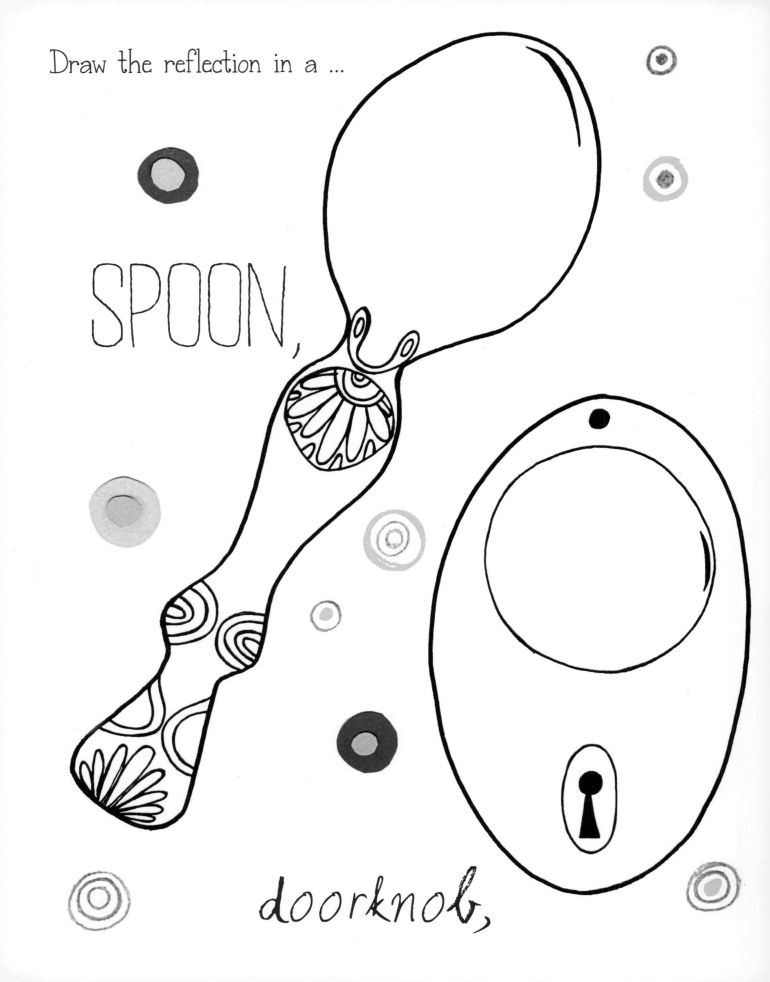

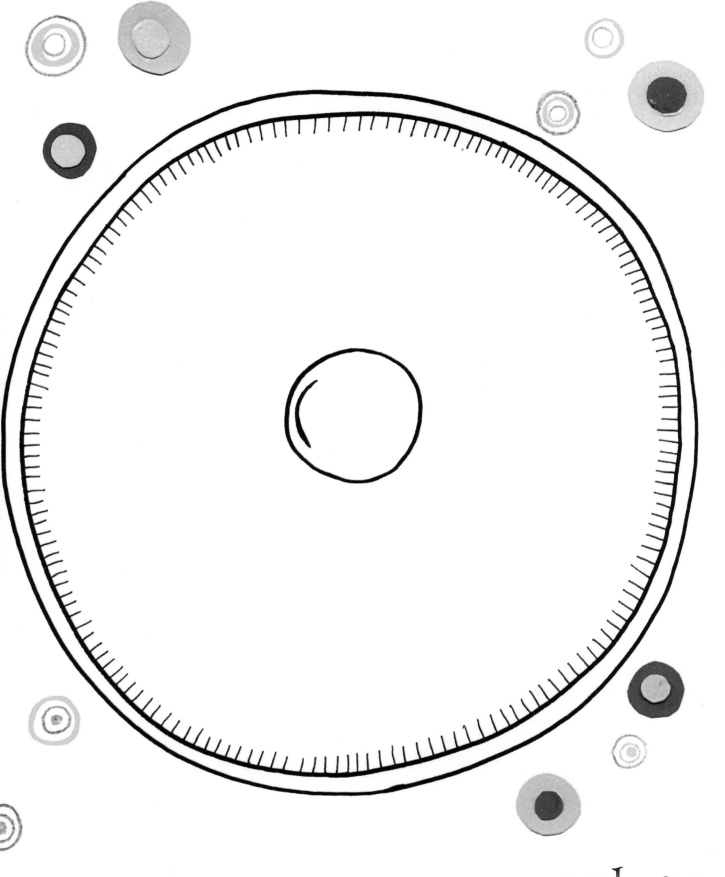

and hubcap.

Draw animals
and their offspring.

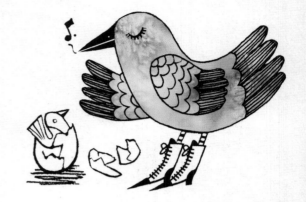

cat/kitten

dog/puppy

bird/chick

horse/foal

frog/tadpole

kangaroo/joey

cow/calf

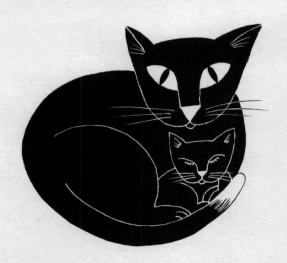

Draw the perfect weather.

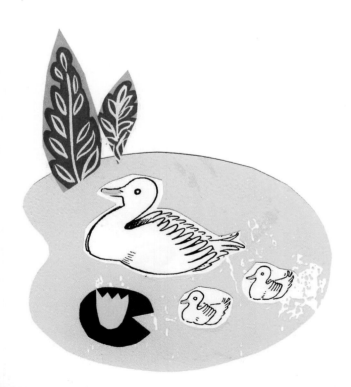

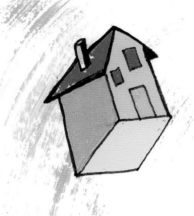

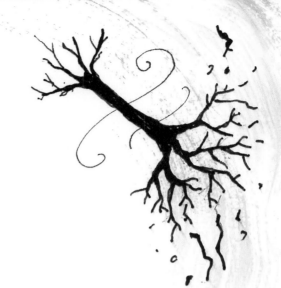

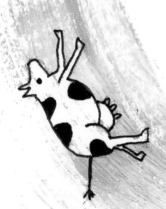

Draw the eye of
the STORM.

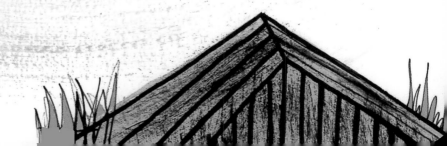

Fill this jar

WITH DICE.

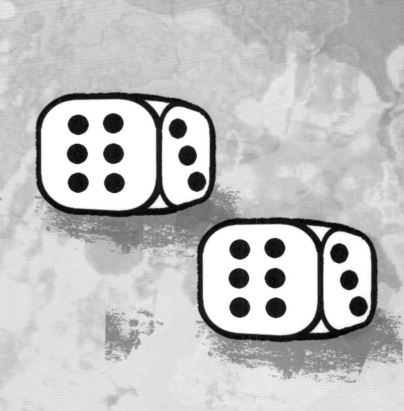

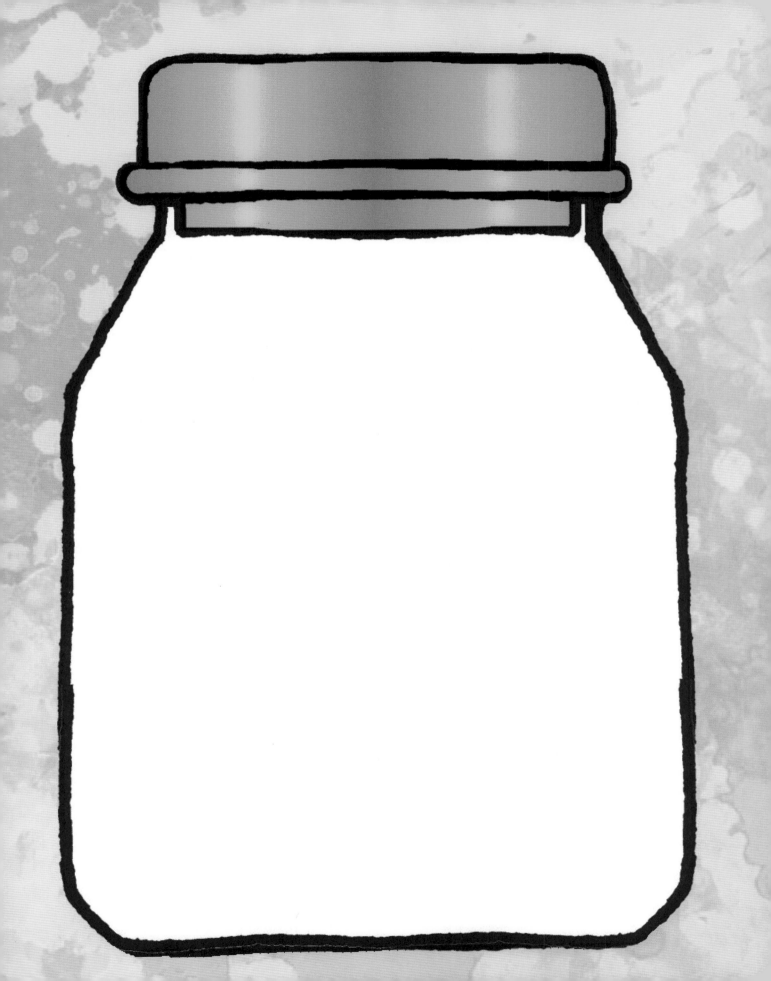

Draw something SPIKY.

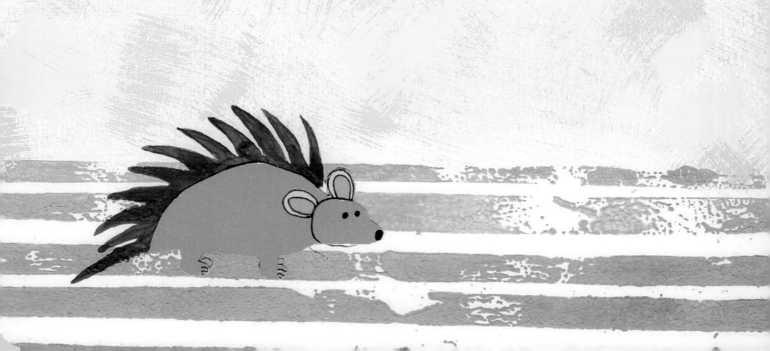

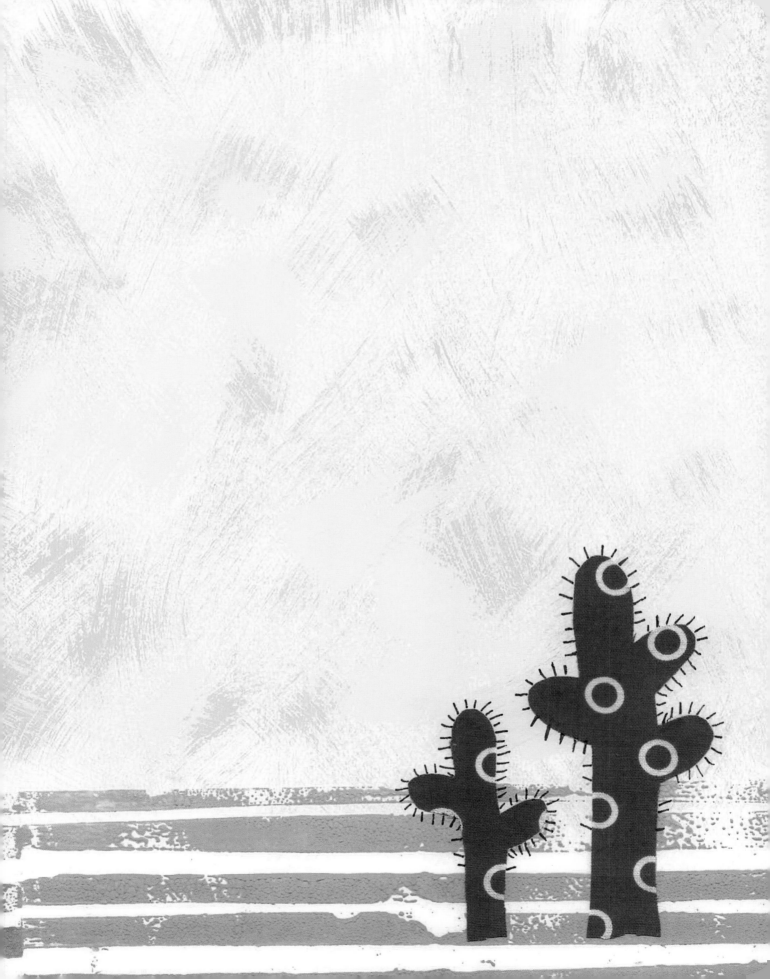

Draw ...

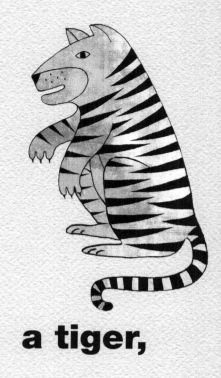

a tiger,

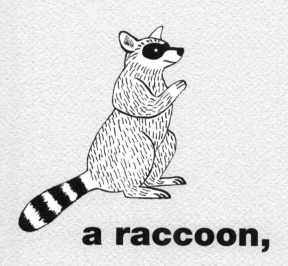

a raccoon,

and an eagle.

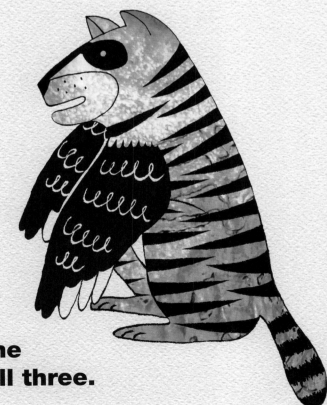

**Now draw one
image of all three.**

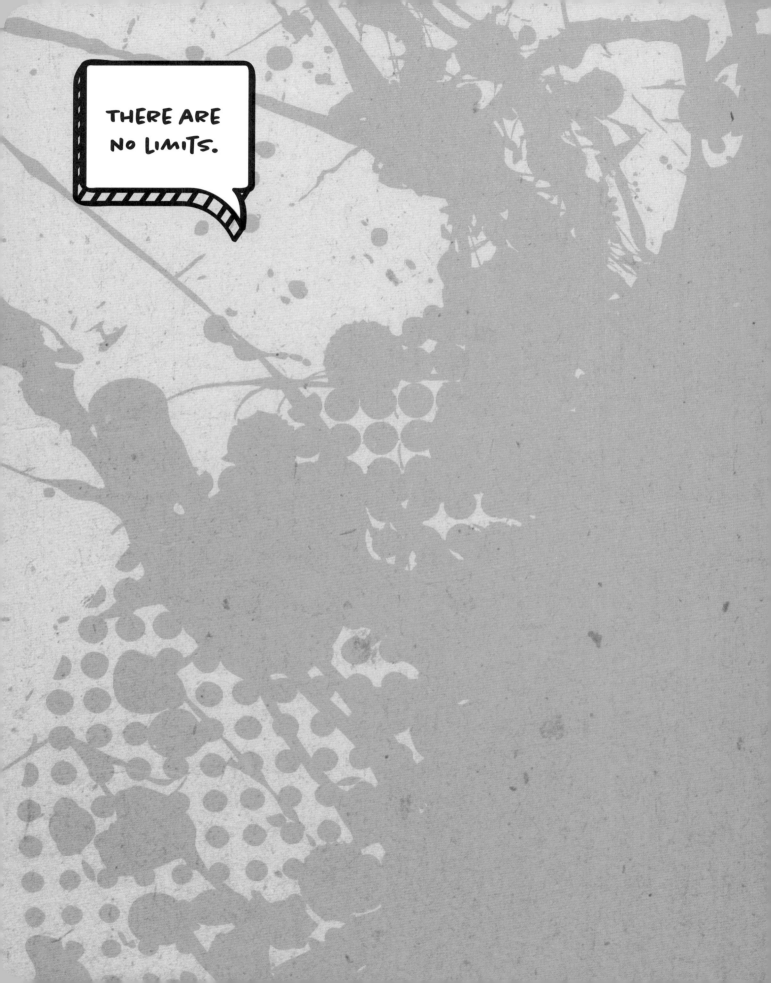

Draw the songs or music coming from around this campfire.

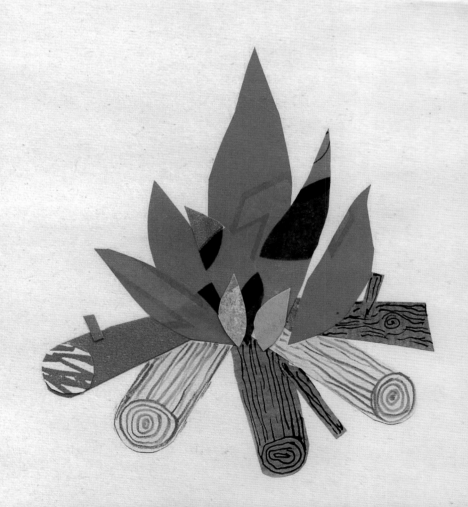

Turn these
shapes into faces
and give them each a different emotion.

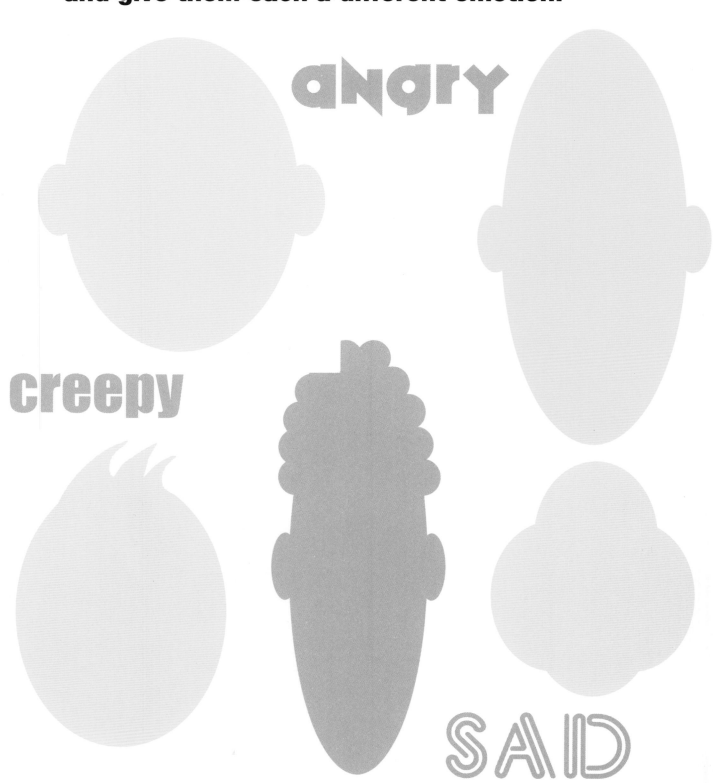

angry

creepy

SAD

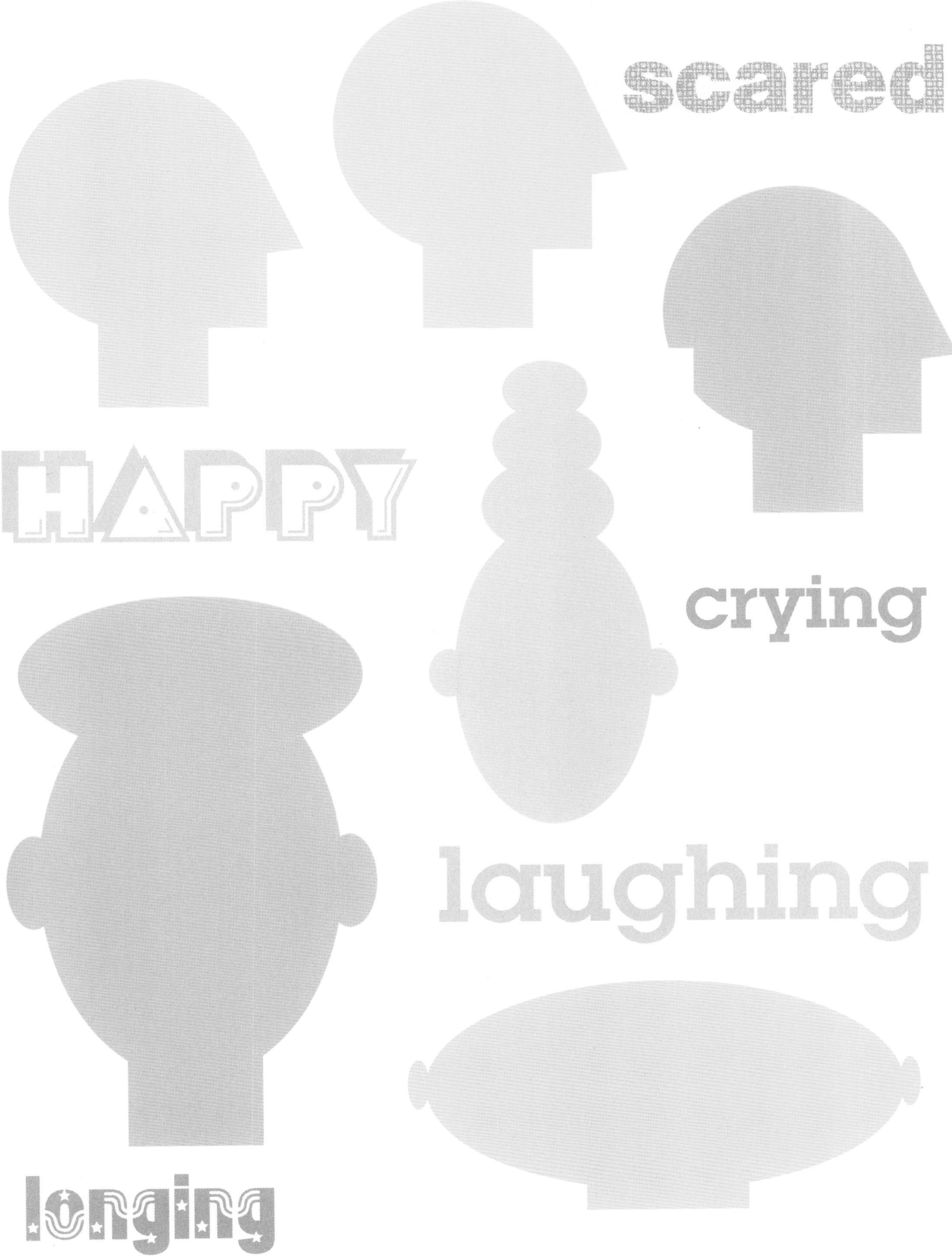

scared

HAPPY

crying

laughing

longing

Draw a landscape.

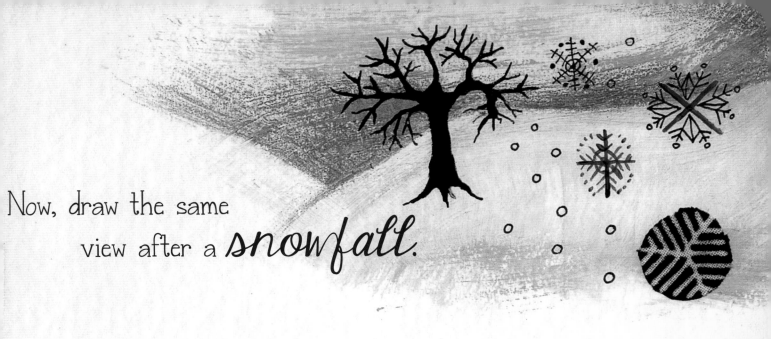

Now, draw the same view after a *snowfall*.

Fill these pages with a
BUSY CROWD
of people.

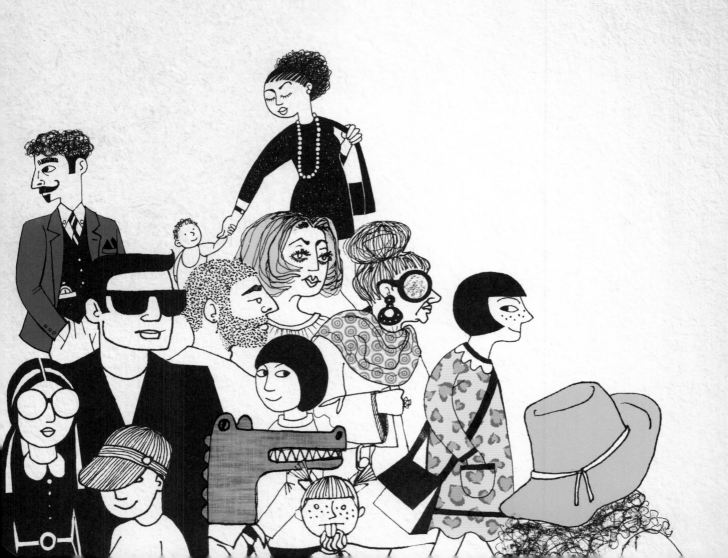

Fill this whale shape with BLUE creatures.

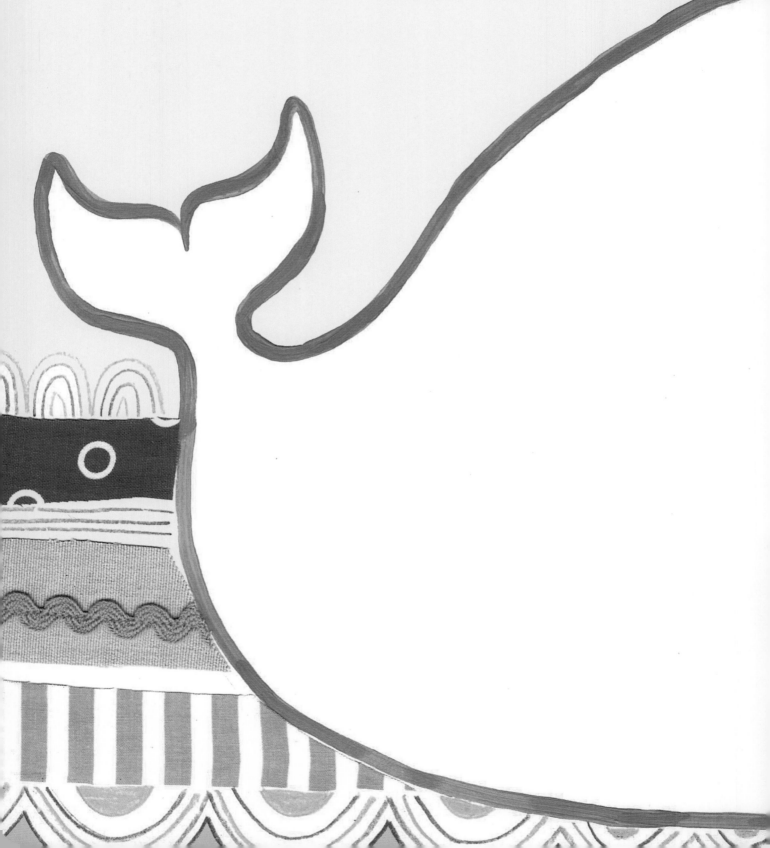

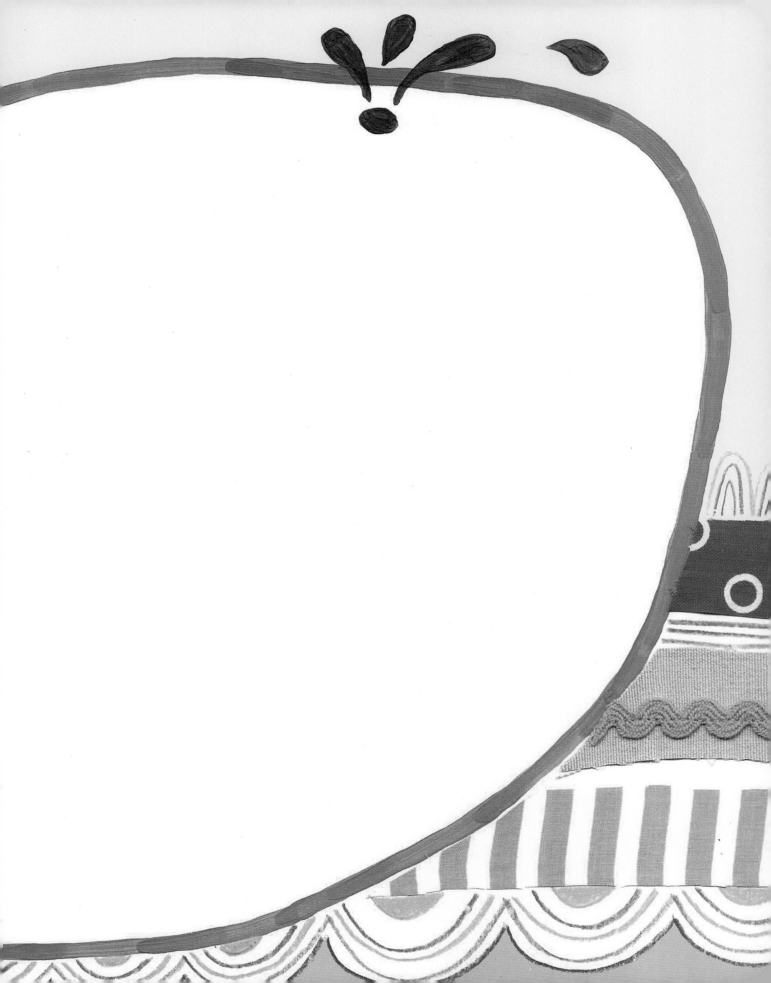

Draw your

FAVORITE DISH

coming out of this oven.

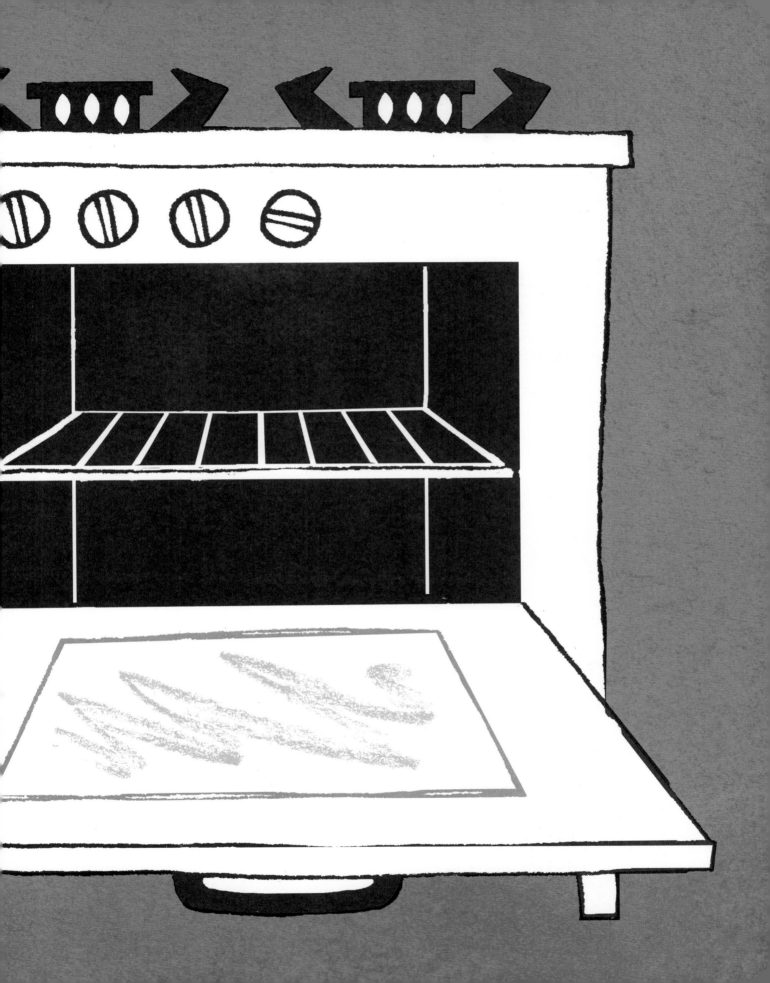

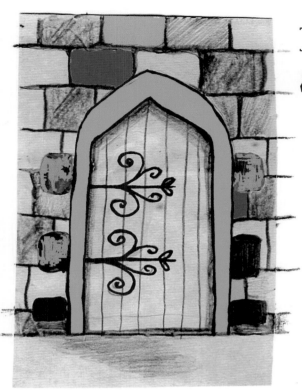

Draw an
ancient doorway.

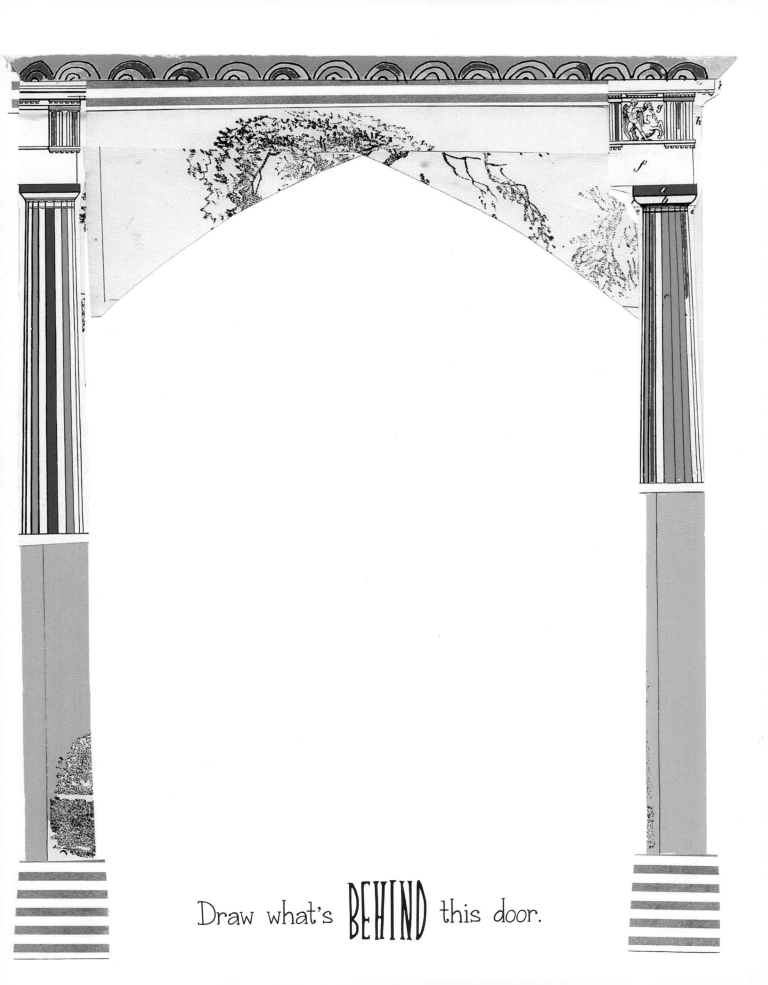

Draw what's BEHIND this door.

Design a **jazzy pattern** for these socks.

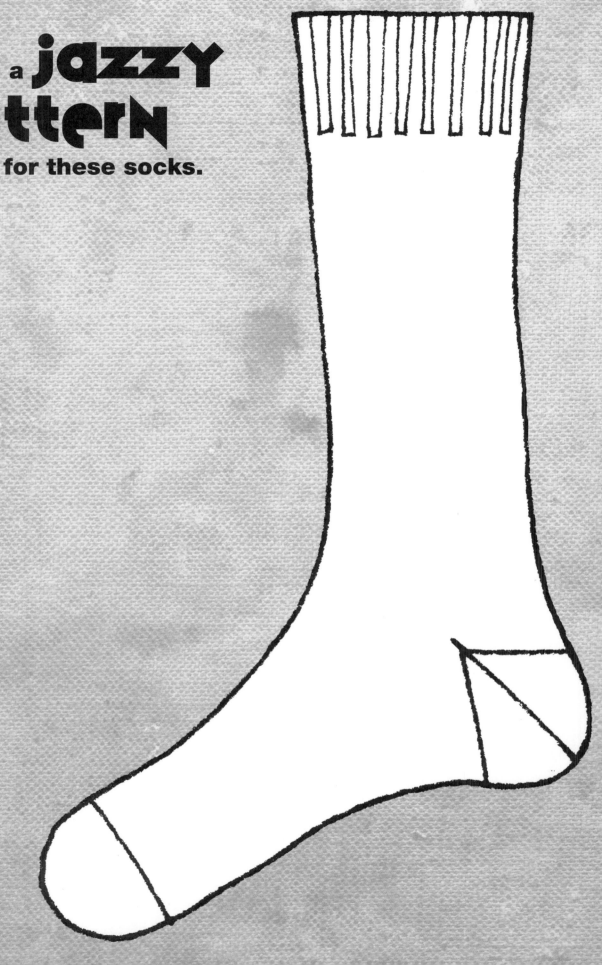

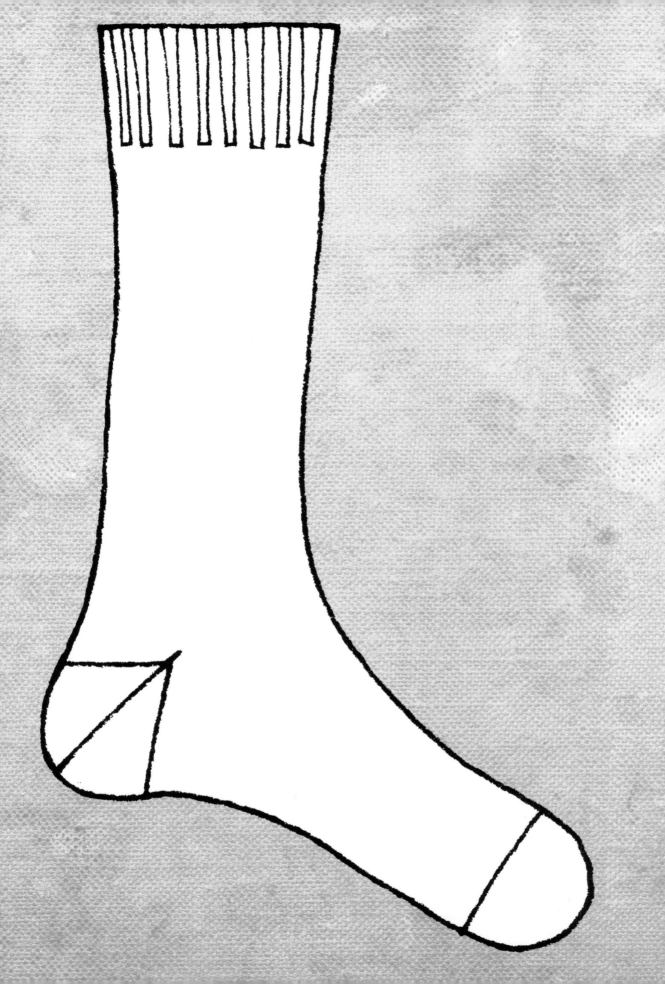

Draw a **dreamy** color.

Draw a **petrified** color.

Draw a **MACHO** color.

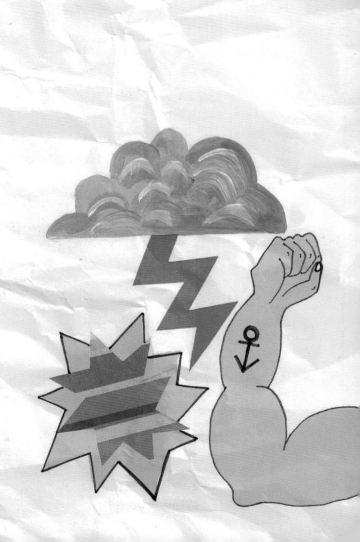

Add someone to this
zip line.

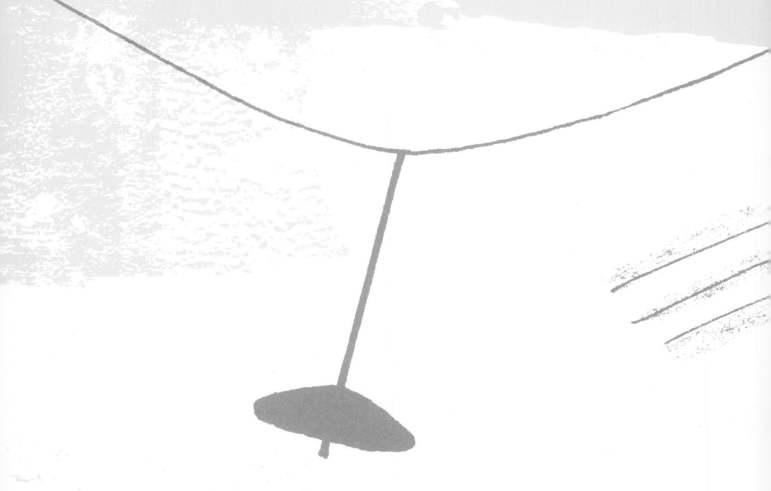

Draw someone
BALANCING
on this tightrope.

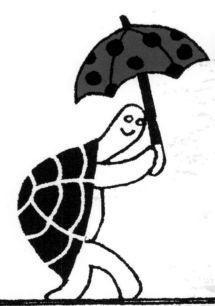

Draw something that is *small*,
but so that it fills this page.

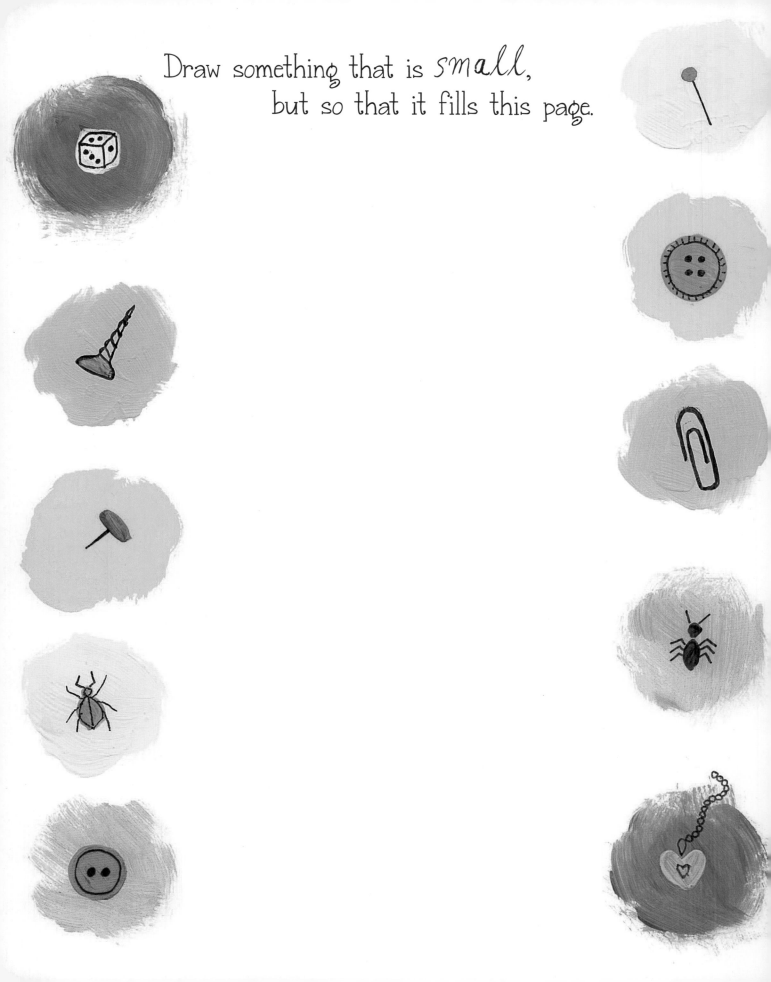

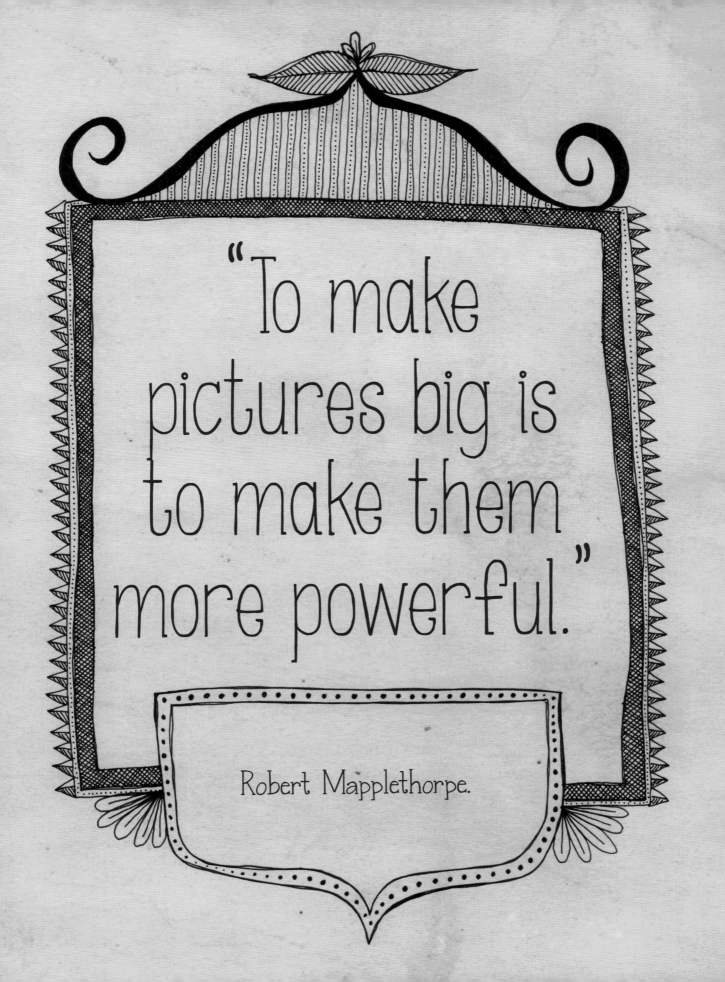

"To make pictures big is to make them more powerful."

Robert Mapplethorpe.

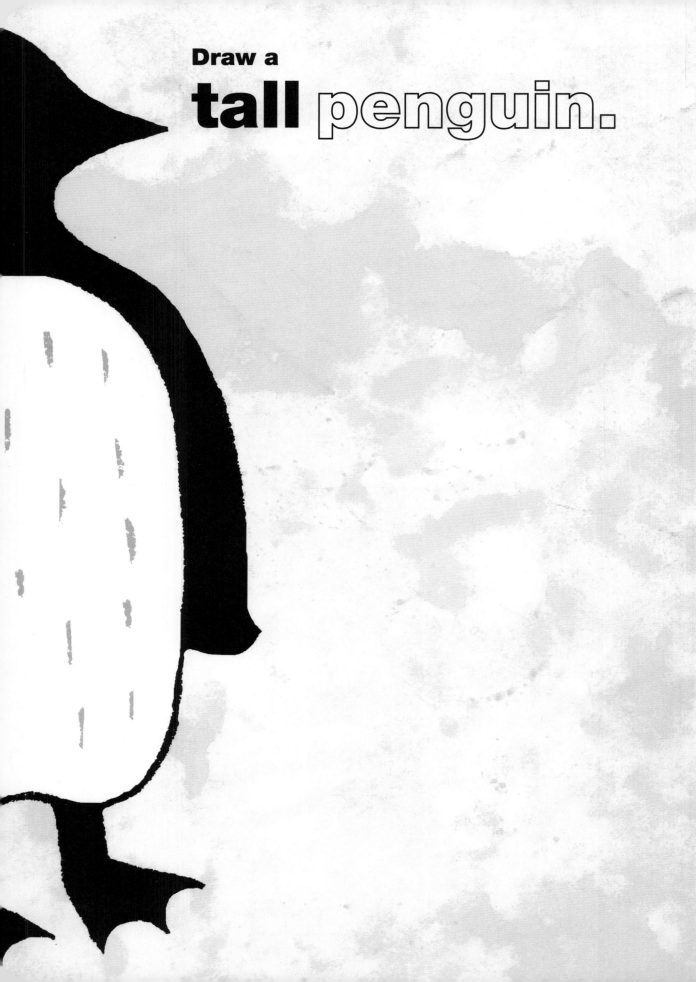

Draw a tall penguin.

Draw a short giraffe.

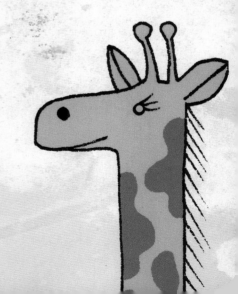

Draw a *cover design* for your all-time favorite book.

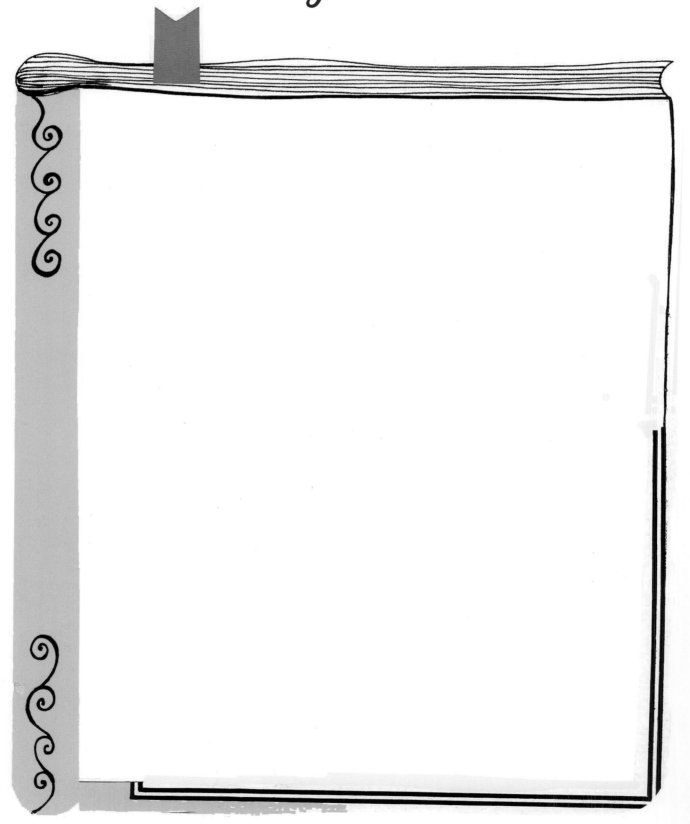

Draw a cover design for your least favorite book.

Can you turn this graph paper into a polka-dot pattern?

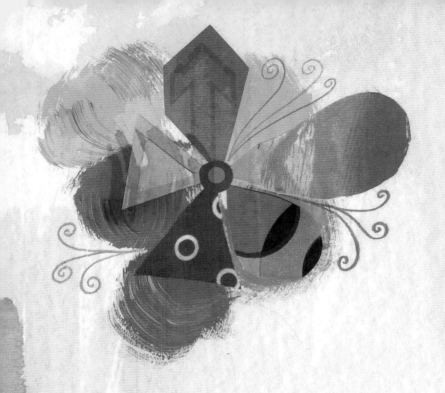

Write a list of words about color.

Can you make those words into an *abstract* piece of art?

Add some frosting
to these cupcakes.

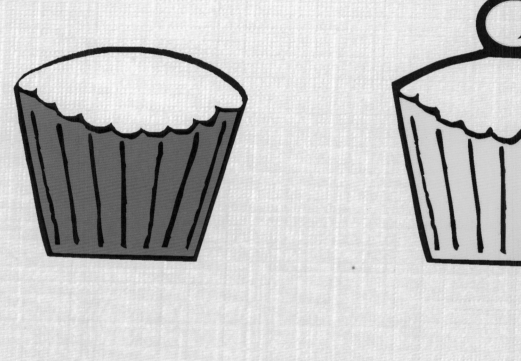

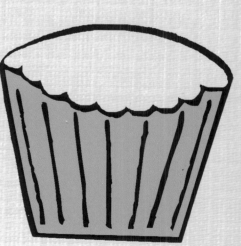

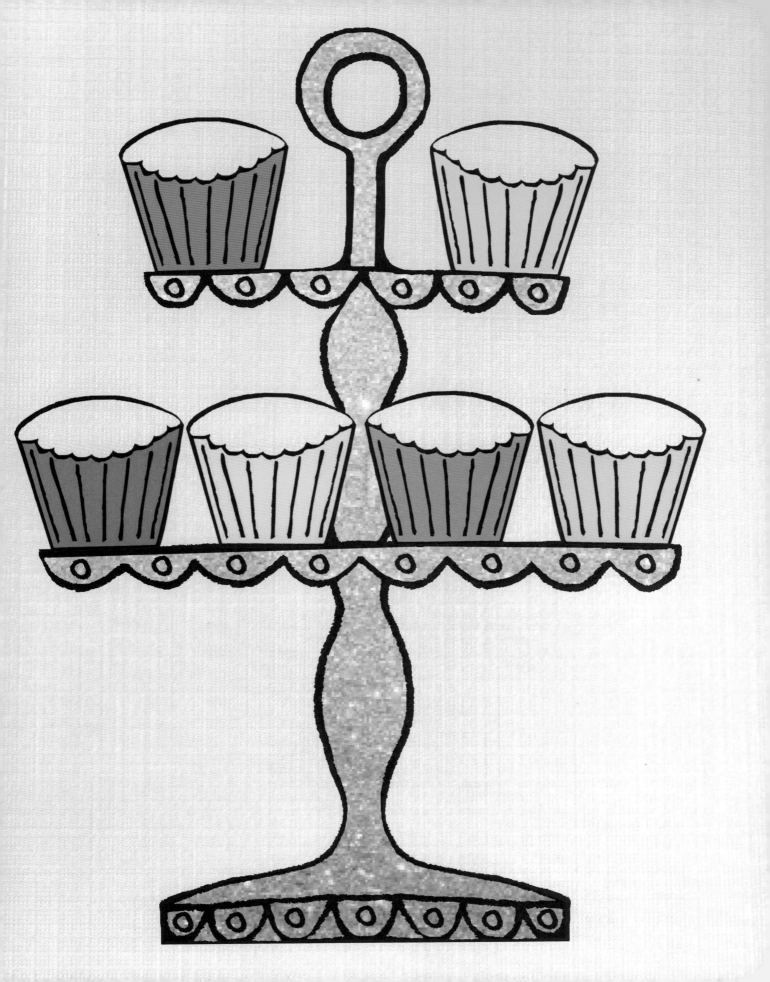

Draw what is in this SUITCASE.

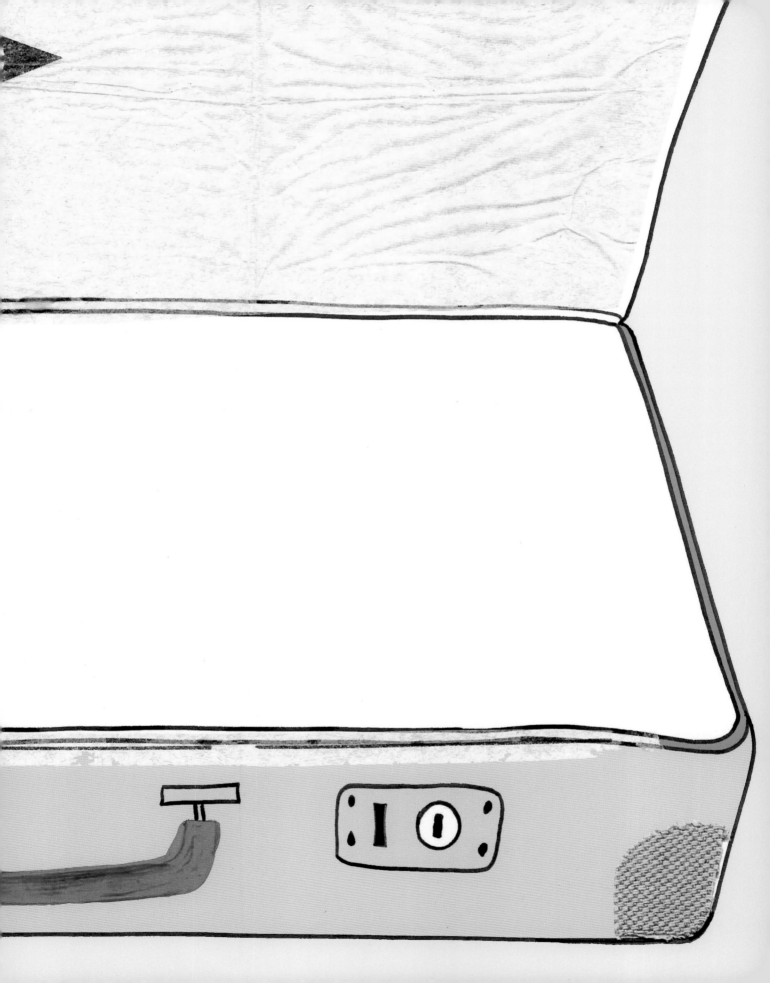

Add
SKATEBOARDERS
to this skate ramp.

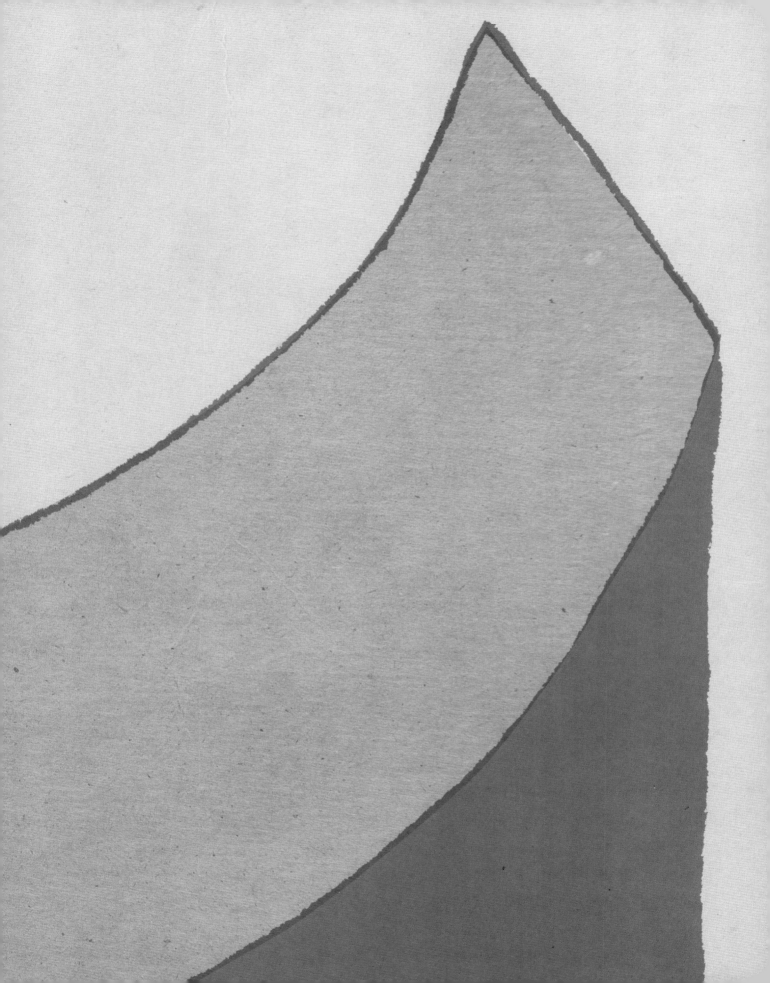

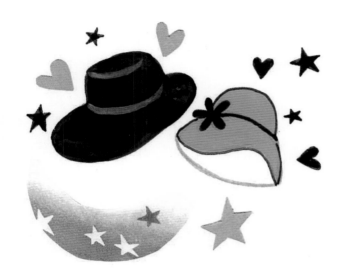

Draw *pink* and **black** in love.

Draw an argument between
yellow and ORANGE.

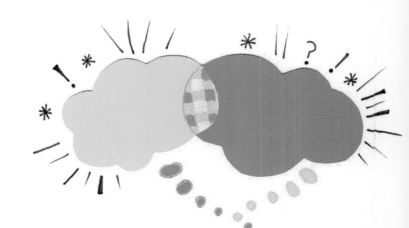

Draw *burgundy* and TURQUOISE dancing and spinning.

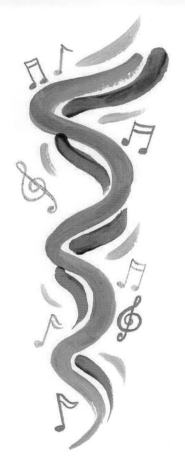

Add some # pinwheels **to the dark.**

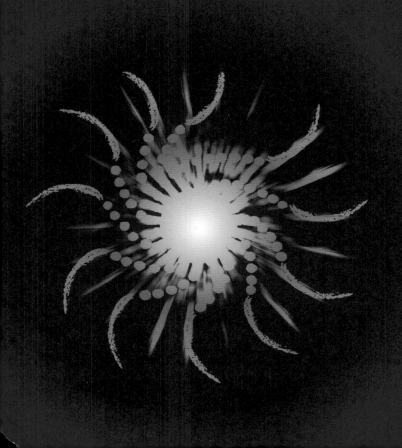

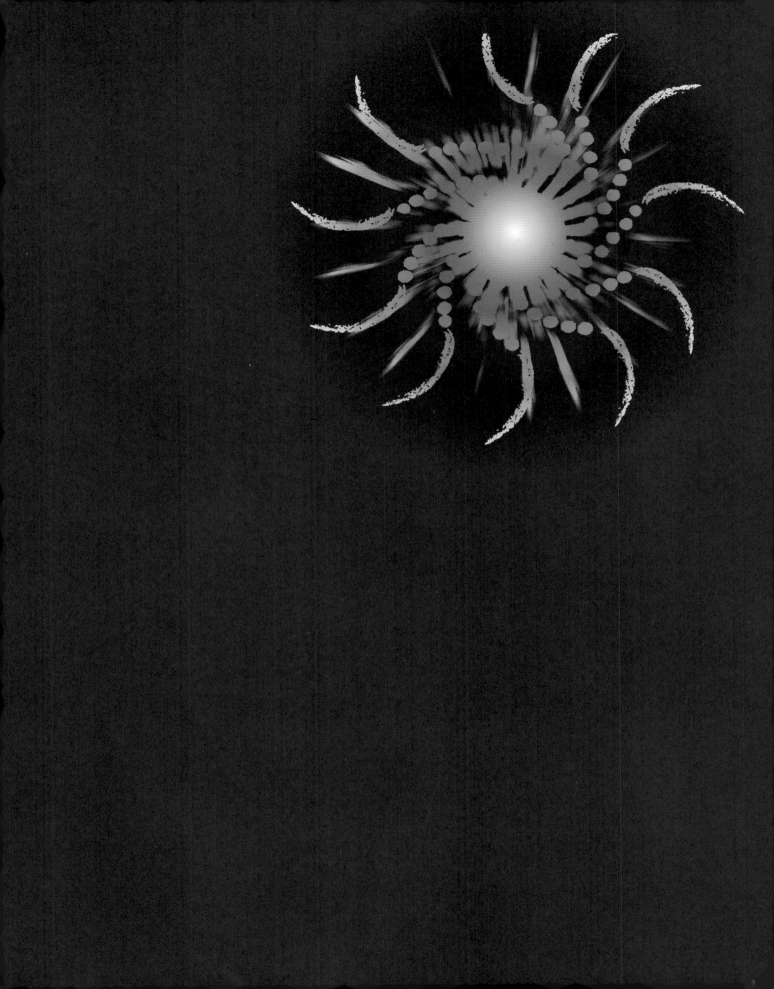

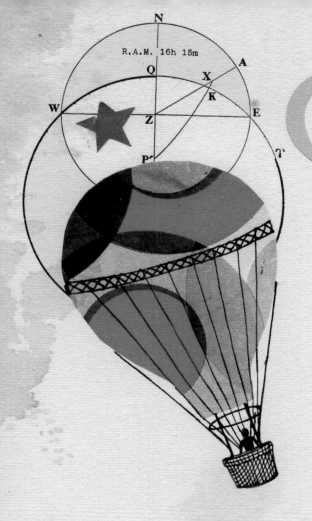

Draw an **aerial view** of where you are.

Create a pattern using

four colors.

Draw something *scared*-

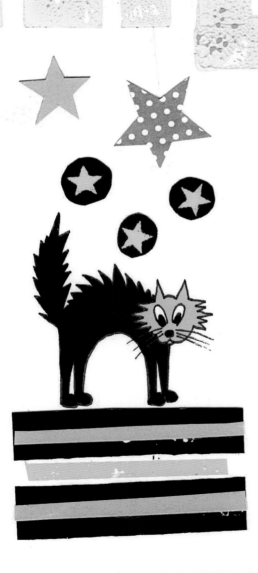

Draw something SCARY.

Draw a self-portrait.

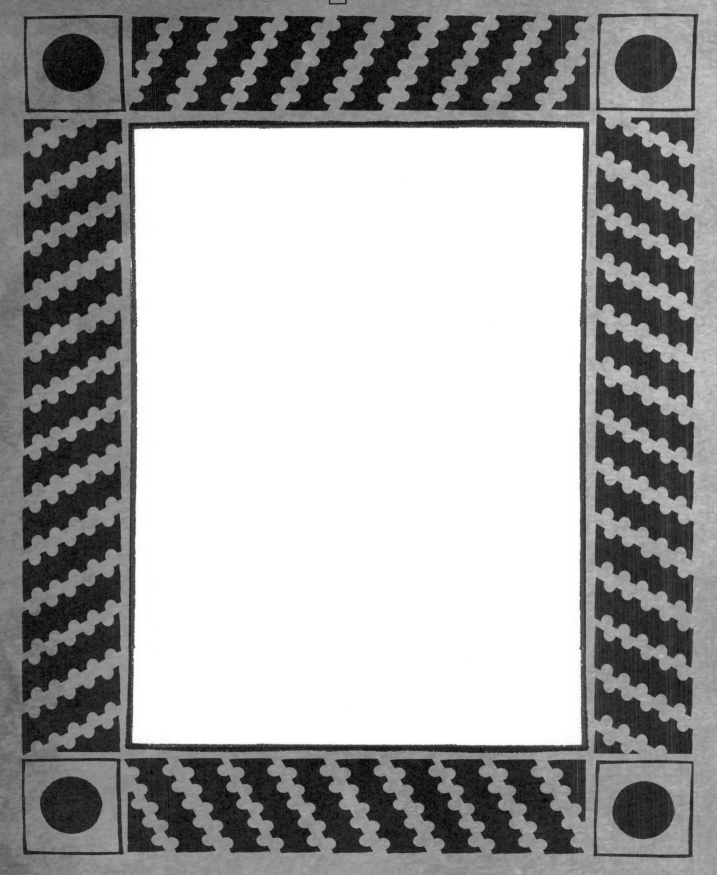

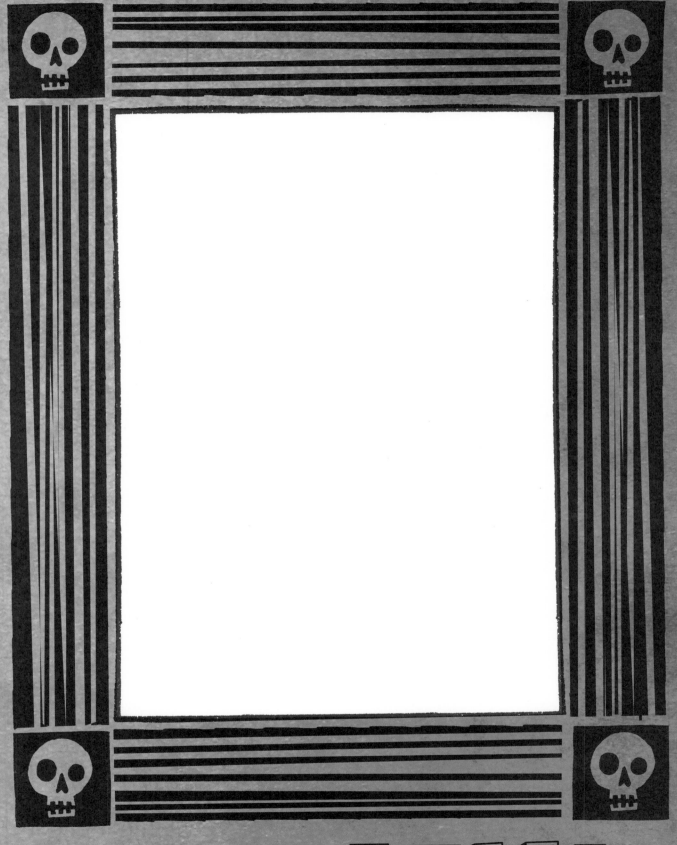

Draw yourself as a ZOMBIE.

Draw something OLD.

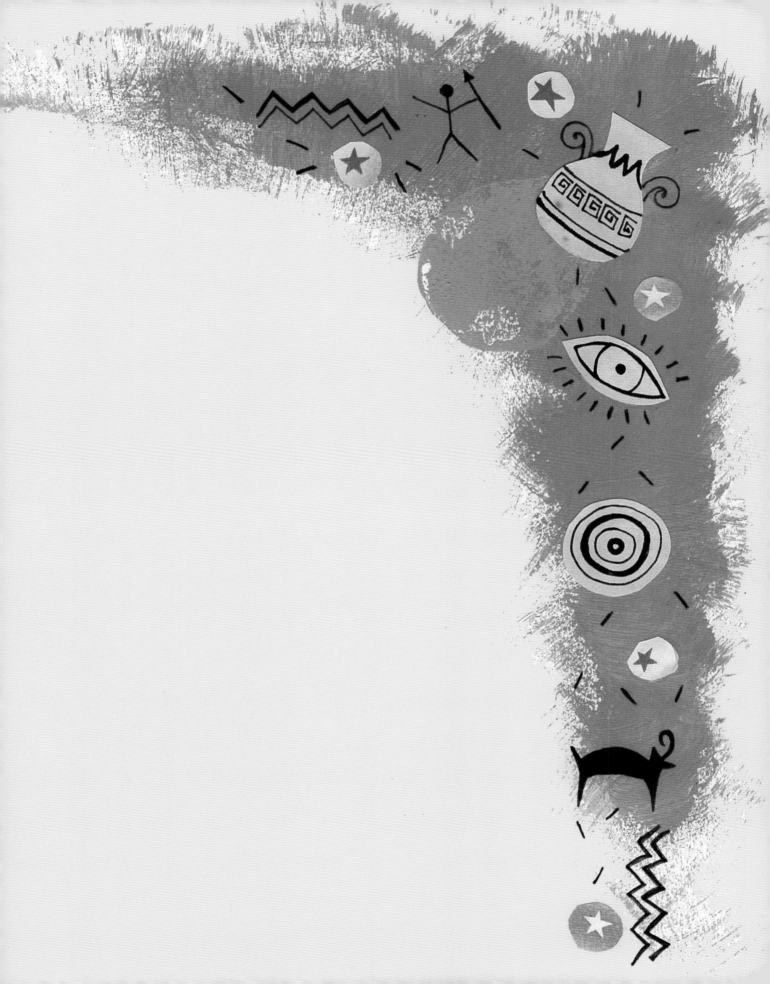

Draw things that have sunk to the bottom of the ocean.

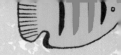
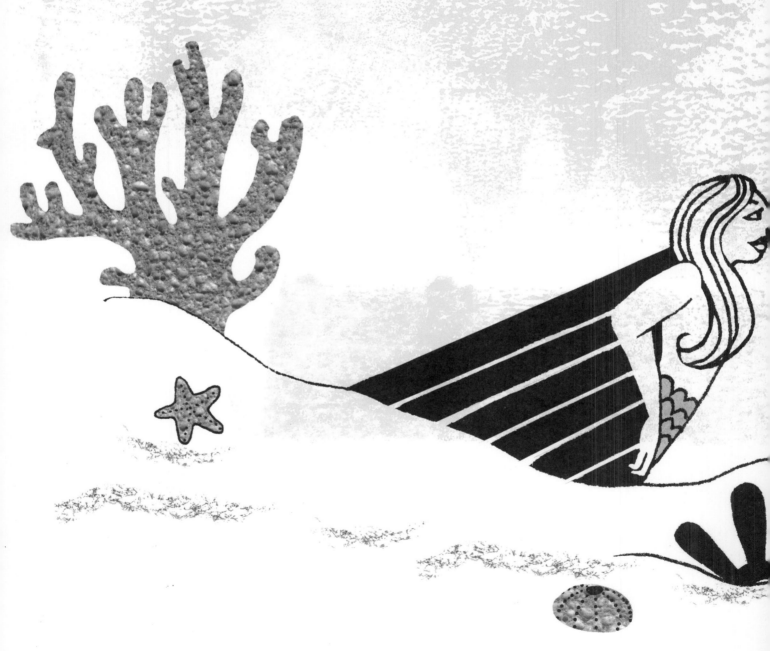

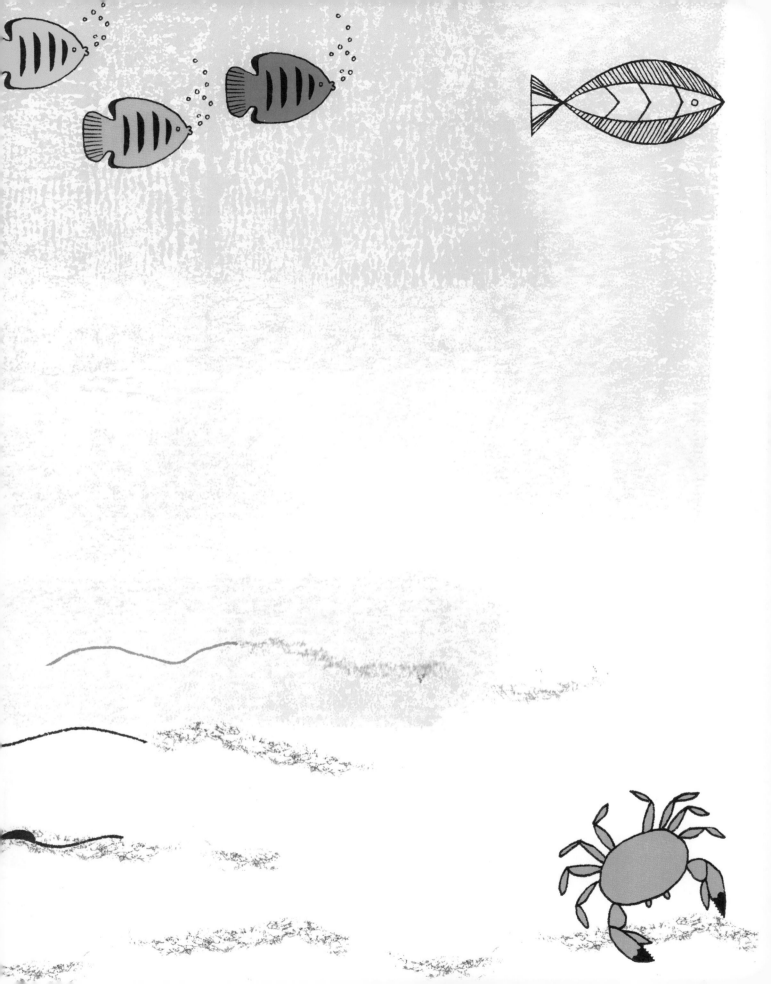

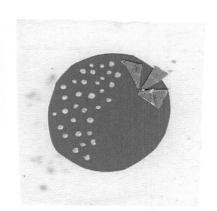

Draw something *soft.*

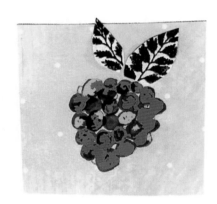

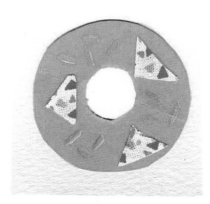

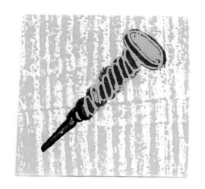

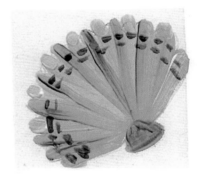

Draw something **hard.**

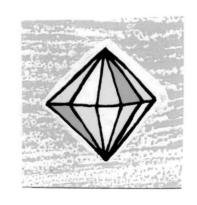

Fill these jars with your
FAVORITE CANDY.

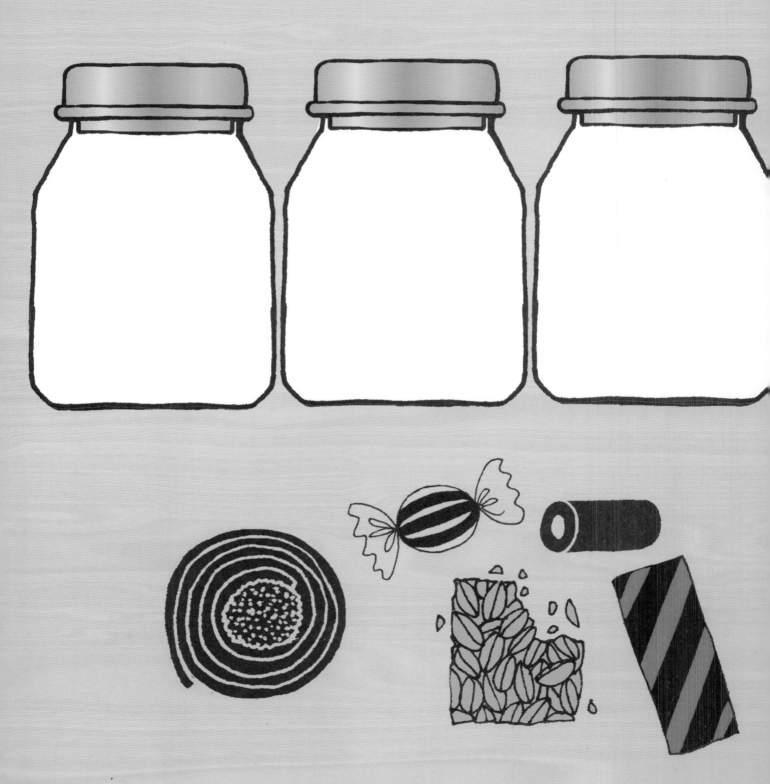

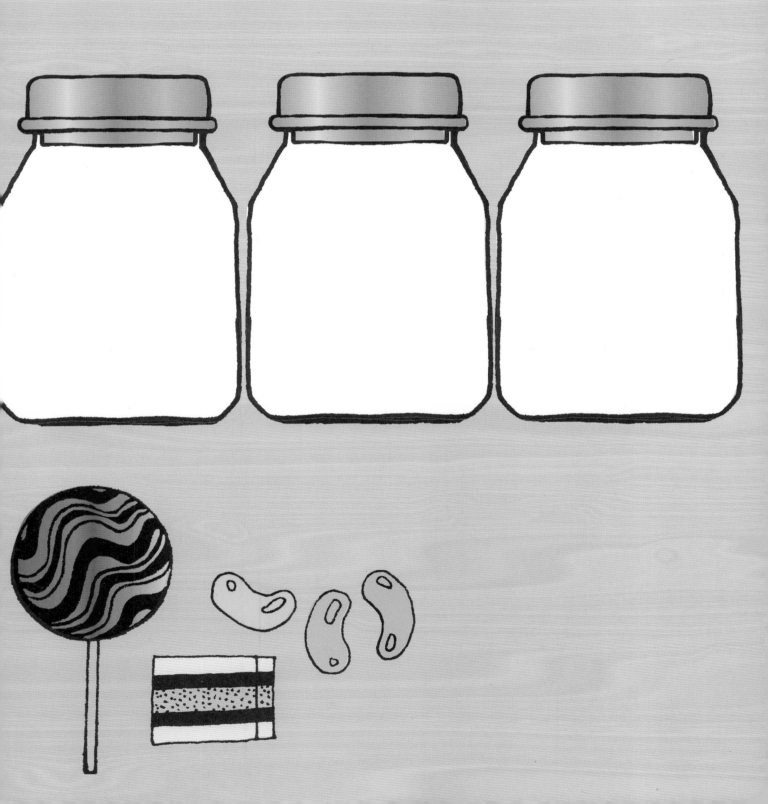

Draw a *rainbow scene* in black and white.

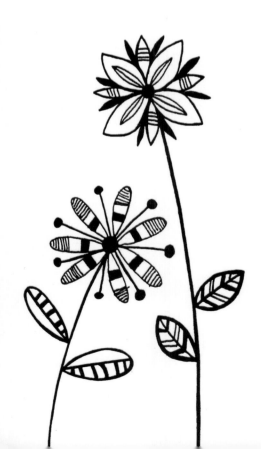

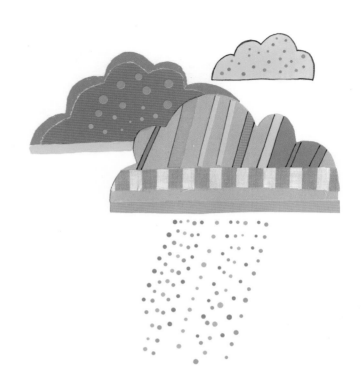

Draw a gray, rainy day using fluorescent colors.

Draw a
FIREFIGHTER
holding this hose.

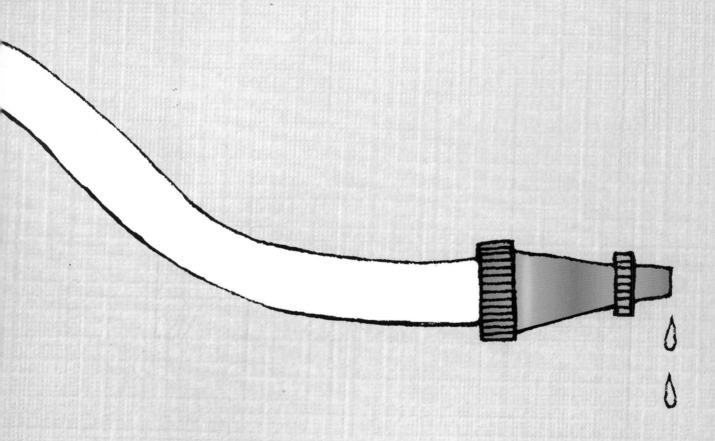

Draw what is on FIRE.

Draw some **witches** flying through this night sky.

Draw a
conversation.

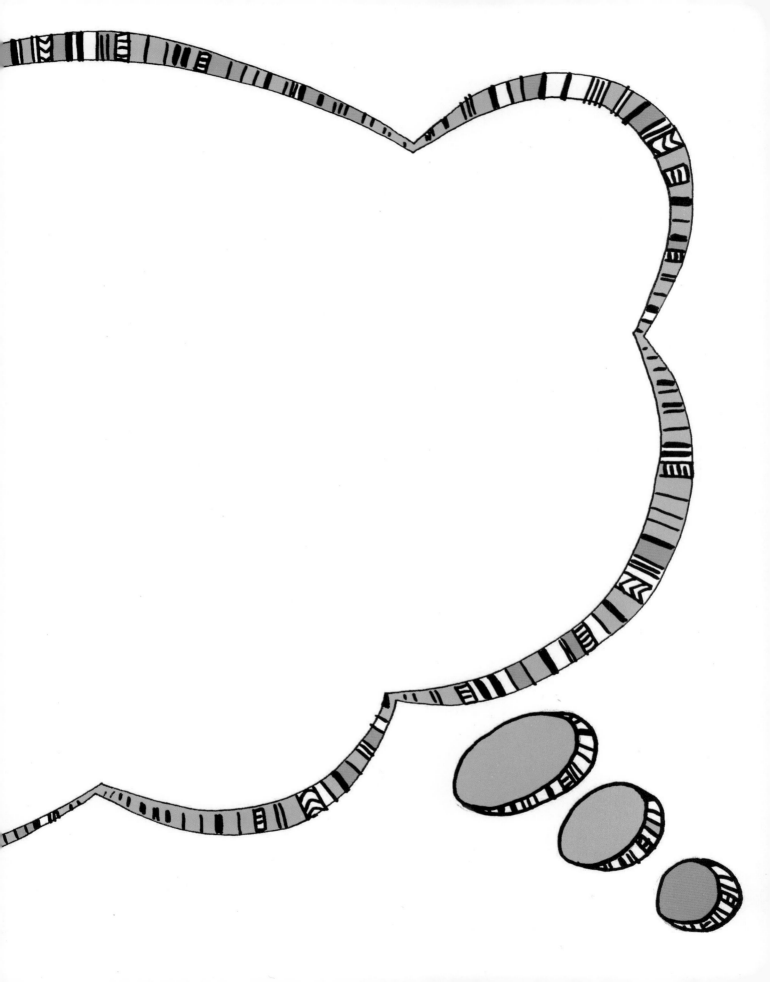

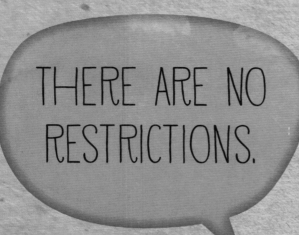

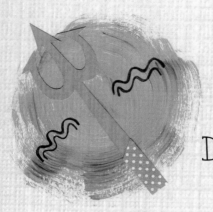

Draw a MYTH.

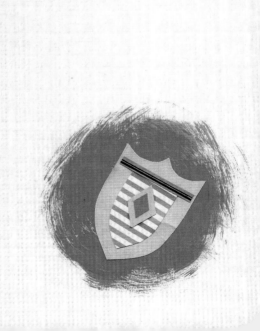

Use as many colors as you can to create an INTRICATE PATTERN.

"Every child
The problem is
an artist once

is an artist-
how to remain
we grow up."

Pablo Picasso.

Add some hats and coats to this
hatstand.

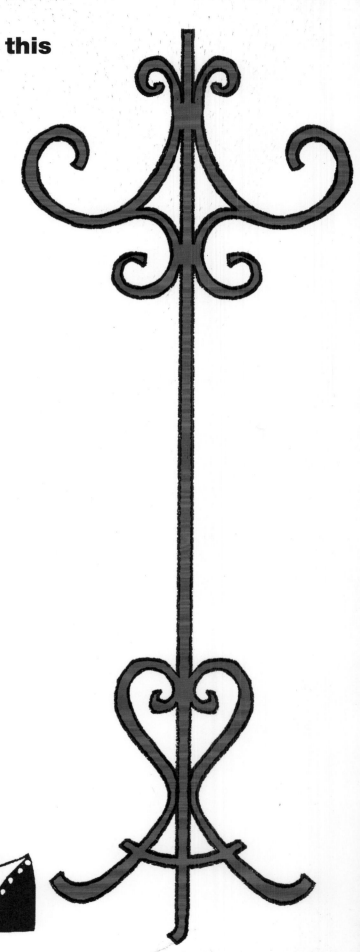

Doodle, IMAGINE, Draw

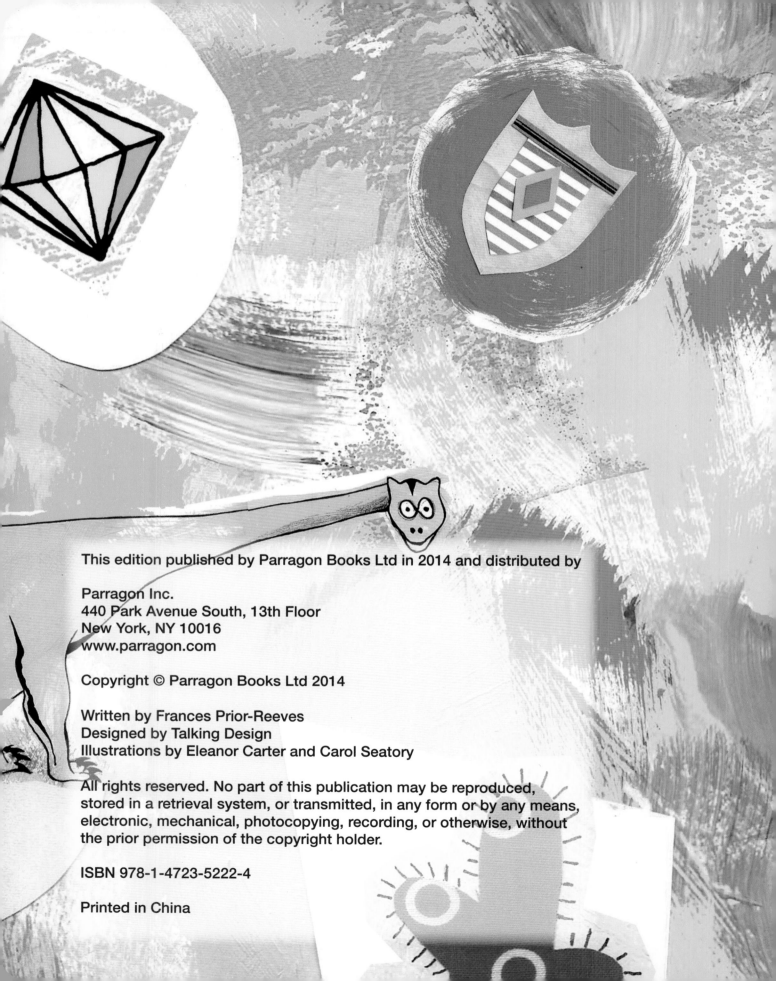

This edition published by Parragon Books Ltd in 2014 and distributed by

Parragon Inc.
440 Park Avenue South, 13th Floor
New York, NY 10016
www.parragon.com

Copyright © Parragon Books Ltd 2014

Written by Frances Prior-Reeves
Designed by Talking Design
Illustrations by Eleanor Carter and Carol Seatory

ISBN 978-1-4723-5222-4

Printed in China